Age 21

Where Mistakes & Magic Happen

Authors Tree®
PUBLISHING

Authors Tree Publishing

{W/16, Aman Vihar, KBT MIG, Bilaspur, Chhattisgarh 495001
First Published By Authors Tree Publishing 2022}

ISBN: 978-93-91078-22-5
MRP: Rs.275/- | 6 USD

Age 21

Where Mistakes & Magic Happen

By

Himanshu Dipak Pathak

Dedication

Dedicated to the power within all of us- the power to Survive, the power to make comebacks, and the power to win. Most of all for me my mother – who always makes sure to stand by me in all situations. To become the source of light for our family. To my father -who taught me to be on my own and that no matter what you can always have yourself a chance to win. His hard work and sacrifices became a source of motivation for me. To my brother- who always reminds me of my younger self and to be the best – best friend I could ever have. His words have always been a benchmark for my actions.

My grandfather- the person who I always respected and loved the most, the person who thought me to become a better person every day. The unconditional love and support have been an unlimited source of happiness for me. My grandmother- from whom I learned the power of right support and how we should take care of what is ours. My Aunts –have been pillars of support, love, and strength.

My mentor and a guide, the man who trusted me when I was at my Low. The man who taught me the meaning of freedom and contribution. Who helped me to grow as a person and a coach and I owe it to – Mr. Prajesh Trotsky.

A few friends who decided not to give up on me in those hard times and who have been a part of some of the events shared in the Book.

To Preeti Muzumdar- who motivated me to write the book, a friend, a guide, and a big Support.

And lastly, to all those students, participants, and my TLC Sirius & BNI VIJAY Buddies who have been a great companion in this journey of life.

To all who intended good for me.

Author's Note

Each person comes into this world with a specific destiny – he has something to fulfill, some message to be delivered, and some work has to be completed. You are not here accidentally – you are here meaningfully. There is a purpose behind you. The whole intends to do something through you.

- Osho (1931-1990) Indian mystic

I read this continuously 5 to 6 times. And I don't know what ran through my body? What strikes through my mind and I decided "let's do this. " I have always thought about changing and transforming lives. While taking NLP (neuro-linguistic programming) workshop, I always kept 1 real thing in mind "if I can't transform them, I won't charge them. " And I really saw this making a very drastic change in my mindset. The mindset and the thought of "Quality over Quantity", the thought of "Transformation over Just Changing with the flow, "and the thought of "Value over price. "

I never just took any workshop for the sake of money. Because I have always believed in and enjoyed the work I do. I always feel I am blessed to do what I do. As very well said in the above lines by Osho, "we are not here accidentally – we are here meaningfully. " So from here, I will believe that this book which I am writing – the techniques and experiences I am going to share with you will not only help you, but also will be your guide for being happy, and getting to the meaning of your being here.

Each person comes into this world with a specific destiny – he has something to fulfill, some message to be delivered, and some work has to be completed. You are not here accidentally – you are here meaningfully. There is a purpose behind you. The whole intends to do something through you.

Oh, I can't stop reading this, just imagine we are not here accidentally - we are here meaningfully. And this surely confirms that I am not writing this book accidentally – I am writing this meaningfully. And if I am here to fulfill something - this book is also going to be there to fulfill something.

If there is a purpose behind me – there is a sure purpose behind this book. And I am blessed that this book, the chapter, the experiences, the activities, and the change – are intended to get to you through me.

What a lovely life this is…

This surely gave me Goosebumps, how blessed I am to be the one chosen to pass a few important messages.

Oh wait,

So this also means, "you also are not reading this book accidentally – you are reading it meaningfully. "There is a purpose behind you reading this book. And there is an intention for you through this book.

Oh dear lord, how blessed you are - we are, to be chosen.

But this also raises some questions in my mind, this also makes me think about a lot of day-to-day people I meet, talk to, and cross paths with.

Each person comes into this world with a specific destiny – he has something to fulfill, some message to be delivered, and some work has to be completed. You are not here accidentally – you are here meaningfully. There is a purpose behind you. The whole intends to do something through you.

If all these lines are true, then are we really doing what we are supposed to do?

Like I met a guy a few days back, who accepted to be that he is addicted to alcohol. So is he destined to be an alcoholic? Is it the meaning of his life?

Like a girl who came to me saying I broke up with my guy, now I won't marry anyone. Is she destined to be alone? What exactly is the message that God wants to pass through?

What about that couple who didn't fight for their relationship? Was it not their work to be completed?

And what about that couple who fought a lot of battles just to get divorced right in 3 to 4 years? What did they fulfill?

Oh, all these questions, just like chattering monkeys started troubling my mind. What is your say in all this?

If we all are destined and are here to deliver a message. Are you on a path to fulfillment?

Is your thought helping you to fulfill your purpose?

Are your values helping you to deliver the right message?

Did your actions serve the right intentions?

What work, important work did you complete to add value to the universe?

And if we all are here with a meaning,

Just ask yourself,

Are you here to be broken?

Mentally disturbed?

In debt?

Just to pay EMI?

Just to wait for someone who may be doesn't value you?

Or to end the life for something or someone who left you when you needed them the most?

Are you here to be known as an alcoholic, druggist, or untrustworthy?

I am sure you yourself have answered all these questions. Because yes, when I read the above lines, I took the charge of my life. And I decided that I am here to write this book, to change and transform peoples' lives, to be called a change-maker, to be a hero in someone else's life, to enjoy good wealth, to enjoy relations – relations that serve loyalty and love in my life.

I am here to make that dent in the universe that Steve Jobs was talking about. I am here to pass the message of self-healing through my words and my dear friend most importantly

"I am here for you " and this book here " to be your friend – a guide for your mind, a mind map for your goals, a mentor for the child inside you, and the missing piece of your puzzle."

So now I hope you have also realized that you are not here accidentally – but meaningfully.

It is time for you to unlock the purpose of your life, the intention of being here.

We as human beings are actually blessed to find our purpose in life while living each day and we are also blessed that we can change it, mould it, and transform it through our actions.

But here the first thing you got to ask yourself is " do you trust that you are destined to be great " or do you think you are here to be average.

Being average is not bad. There is nothing wrong with being average. Average people keep the country moving. Average is okay and completely acceptable in society. But if you want to be different, if you want to change, then you must prepare yourself to make that commitment to achieve.

We, as we tend to complicate situations doubt a lot, sometimes on ourselves-our destiny-our being here, and our purpose.

So here I have something worth reading, which changed my tendency of complaining and cry over things or situations that didn't go my way.

The Ant & the Contact Lens:

A true story

Brenda was almost halfway to the top of the tremendous granite cliff. She was standing on a ledge where she was taking a breather during this, her first rock climb. As she rested there, the safety rope snapped against her eye and knocked out her contact lens.

'Great', she thought. 'Here I am on a rock ledge, hundreds of feet from the bottom and hundreds of feet to the top of this cliff, and now my sight is blurry.'

She looked and looked, hoping that somehow it had landed on the ledge. But it just wasn't there.

She felt the panic rising in her, so she began praying. She prayed for calm, and she prayed that she may find her contact lens.

When she got to the top, a friend examined her eye and her clothing for the lens, but it was not to be found. Although she was calm now that she was at the top, she was saddened because she could not clearly see across the range of mountains.

She Prayed to God......'Oh, God! You can see all these mountains. You know every stone and leaf, and you know exactly where my contact lens is. Please help me.'

A little later, another set of Hikers reached the top. One of them shouted out, 'Hey, you guys! Did anybody lose a contact lens?'

Well, that would be startling enough, but you know why the climber saw it?

An ant was moving slowly across a twig on the face of the rock, carrying it!

The story doesn't end there. Brenda's father is a cartoonist. When she told him the incredible story of the ant, the prayer, and the contact lens, he drew a cartoon of an ant lugging that contact lens with the caption,

'God I don't know why you want me to carry this thing.

I can't eat it, and it's awfully heavy. But if this is what you want me to do, I'll carry it for you.'

I think it would do all of us some good to say, "God, I don't know why you want me to carry this load. I can see no good in it and it's awfully heavy. But, if you want me to carry it, I will."

God doesn't call the qualified, He QUALIFIES those He calls.

Kindly write your learning from the above story.

....

....

....

....

....

As I mentioned, I strongly feel that I am here to pass some important messages through this book, through the workshops I take and the talks I deliver. I also believe that "WORDS" have some great power in them. Our words can change a person's life, in both ways. Our words can break or can make someone's life. We, with the power of words, can lift someone, and can also give them a ride to hell. And as we all know it is difficult sometimes to be kind and gentle with people if we ourselves are going through times we feel are tough for us.

While writing this to you I don't really know what time of my life is? Is this the part where I am happily enjoying each moment or I am worried about things that are happening to me or with me? But one thing I am sure of is that I am "growing, developing and also contributing. "

This reminds me "What happens in our life doesn't bother us if we take the negative power from it. "

So from here on, we both -yes we both will continue to cut the negative thought of wilderness and "What will happen next?" for a while and we will just feel, what we are feeling at this very moment, and let's just keep moving forward.

How this book can help you?

W elcome my friend, now as you have read the reason why I wrote this book?

It is time for you to understand how this book can overall help you to understand and connect with yourself and how you can use your mistakes to make a fortune out of it. When I say mistakes- and fortune together, a lot of participants during my workshops ask me, "how we can even connect these two words MISTAKES - FORTUNE without worrying about the consequences we have faced because of all those mistakes. What about how we felt, the people we lost, the money we lost, or the emotional baggage we are carrying because of all this?"

So here my friend is a simple example for you to understand what exact message I want to deliver through this book.

But before that, I want you to write your current age in the below Circle. Yes, the age you are reading this book at. Because this is the age you are where your thoughts have the most power over the life you are living. The way you are getting promoted or making a profit. The way you are enjoying or suffering your relationships. Because right now is the age you are, what you have become because of the mistakes you have done in the past.

Now just for a while let us consider our progress decade-wise, so that we can actually have a trip to memory lane, a trip to our past -just to acknowledge it. Because however, it has been -good or bad, easy or hard as some say – fair or unfair as some complain." IT WAS OUR OWN PAST -and it has its own MAGIC in it."

Timeline no.1 (age 1 to 10)

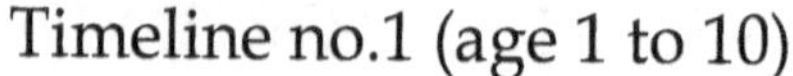

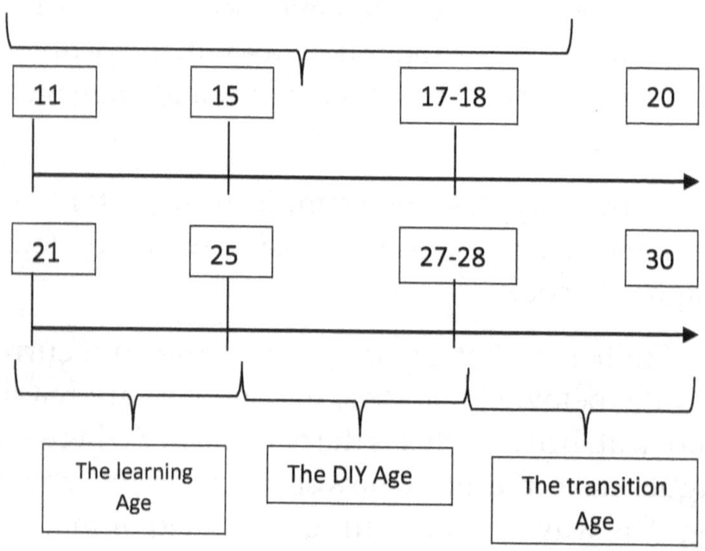

Timeline no.1 (age 1 to 10)

The Learning age - The learning age (I can say don't miss the learnings, but understanding our mind

& human tendency. You will and must have missed a lot of learnings. Here just try to visit them. Don't think out results, just visit the learning this age had for you, yes it may be sometimes difficult to understand the learnings while actually living the situation or a part of life. But it has always been easy for you to connect the dots later on. So now it is again easy for you to connect the dots of all the what? When? Why? And how? Which were running in your mind all this time. **Just de-clutter your mind on a blank page before you actually move towards the next section**.

Now there is a very funny thing about the learning age – "you will always feel you know everything "about whatever you are doing and feeling. But then again "is it really possible for us to know or understand everything?"

Now I know you have answered the question, so the next time you feel that you have it all sorted, stop that thought then and there itself. Shift your energy from assumptions to possibilities. Start thinking about the possibilities in the situation or else our mind has a weird power to assume things from our past references.

So, from here on consciously decide that you will choose possibilities over assumptions. Or else your mind has already decided to take a train to the city of "PAST REFERENCEs. "

I repeat "POSSIBILITIES OVER ASSUMPTION "because my friend you don't know everything, and believe me, "IT'S A BLESSING. "

Just de-clutter your mind on a blank page before you actually move towards the next section.

The DIY Age - Here is the most important part. The part where Implementation comes into the picture and let me already tell you, my friend, this is the Age we will be doing a lot of mistakes. Because we all know while the learning age, we were also busy in making relationships, we were also getting influenced by people and a lot of external factors such as "the idiot box," the so-called "smartphone" (as nowadays kids get exposed to gadgets at a very early age"). And also let us face this, we are wired to our phones. You were also busy enjoying the moment even if it was not meant for you, you were partying, you were in fear sometimes, you were worrying, and you were busy – in being "not busy."

So here you will do a lot of mistakes. Here you will feel uselessness, hopelessness, and unworthy, and sometimes you will also feel "all these things happening with you are accidents happening with you. "

And that's pretty normal, that's why I said earlier we are blessed to do mistakes and learn from them.

Just imagine a deer or a beautiful zebra in a jungle. Their one mistake can directly lead from being a beautiful creature to a Meal for others.

Isn't it a heartbreak?

But we, humans, have got the blessing of doing mistakes – learning from them – and then achieve by implementing those learnings in our life for our betterment.

So how would you like to achieve it? By "do it yourself "or by depending on others to do it for you. Because remember one thing "the more you DIY – the more you will progress, the more others do it for you – others will progress you won't.

And as my mentor always used to say to me "either we grow -or we decay "and for each moment "we don't decide and act to grow – we decay. "

The choice is always yours. Because taking decisions at this age is also a DIY thing.

For some, this will be an age full of challenges, heartbreaks, and uncertainty.

But my dear friend, this is exactly the age where you grow, you evolve, and you are in the driving seat of your life (you should be).

So this age is almost a rollercoaster ride. But do not forget to learn from this age too. And most importantly "observe your thoughts."

The more you will do things on your own during this age, the more it will help you to grow.

I bought my first house (where I live with my family) when I was 23. But I was 25 when I understood financial planning.

I had my first relationship when I was 16 – but I understood "how to be happy in a relationship?" when I am 26.

I started my first business when I was 18 -but understood the meaning of firm when I was 24.

So why exactly I shared these details with you? Because my friend during these days when I was doing all the things on my own, I faced my own set of challenges. But today when I connect all the dots, all things "DIY" things actually helped me to progress.

So the more "you do "during this age, the more "you will" grow. So don't be dependent on someone else to fight your battles for you. Don't rely on others to tell you that you are good enough to handle all this. And most importantly don't be a fool to ask others if you are doing this right. Spend time with yourself more often, try to know yourself -things you like, things you don't like. People you love-people you don't like spending your energy with. When you start spending time with the things you like & love -you will start to recognize your self-worth and you will without efforts start maintaining your energy.

I meet a lot of people who are dependent on others to tell them that they have changed, or they are the same person they used to be. These people always think about "what they will think if I do this – or that?" And ultimately at the end of the day, these people become people pleasers. The thought of "what will they think "become so powerful for them that they decide to not do things others don't like. Now here is the catch – these people will make a lot of friends to hang out with, but they feel lonely even if they are with others.

These people don't want to bother others with their actions so they don't do things even if they love to do and enjoy. Their fun depends on others, their feelings depend on others, and their happiness depends on others.

Now ask this question to yourself "have you been doing this?" are you those "OTHER PEOPLE" I am talking about here?

Because let's face the reality "we cannot make everyone happy." Some will love everything we do or say -whereas some won't like anything we do or say to them.

Yes, I must have pissed off a lot of people while being ME, and some must have loved the way I talk, walk, do things, think, and the way I live my life.

The ultimate question we need to answer ourselves is "do we have that free spirit in ourselves to live it out in our own way -or we are going to keep worrying about what they will think?

I have a friend who did his graduation according to his relatives. He does a job he hates doing just because a few of his cousins got the same job when they started their careers. He got married just because his family thought this is a good time for him. Whereas he wanted to complete his PG.

He is now planning to have a child. But every other day he complains about the life he is living-the job he is doing, and the way things have been with him lately. And the most important part here is "he is not happy." Just imagine what kind of quality his life has been and will be if he doesn't stop being a people pleaser. Will he be able to enjoy his job?

Will he be able to fully love his wife?

Will he be able to enjoy each moment during the days his child will grow?

Would he like to remember his life the way he is living it?

I really hope my friend you are not doing this mistake.

Nowadays when I meet people who complain about the government, the environment, the way our country is, or the way we are playing cricket. I understand where they are coming from.

I realized this after addressing more than 1000s of people during my workshops that, "people who criticize others the most are not happy with the life they are living – it is not you whom they are criticizing – it's their own emptiness that drives them to criticize others. I still remember, one day a teacher of mine started shouting at the whole class, I still don't know the reason why she did that. But in the next 10 minutes, she had tears in her eyes while saying "everyone has planned to trouble me. "

Did she mean everyone in the class? Did she mean everyone in the school? Did she mean everyone in the world?

Only she knows the answer. I don't know what she was going through – but there was something that she was not feeling good or comfortable about. And she started venting it in the class.

I also went through something like this back in 2016 when I had gone through a nervous breakdown. I used to feel empty inside, sometimes lost, and always angry at others. I used to feel that everybody except me is doing something that is totally wrong. I started criticizing people, my friends -family, and everybody I used to meet. I used to feel that they are not supporting me. That they are not looking after me. I was always angry with OTHERS for whatever was happening in my life.

Yes, it was the time I felt I am going to go down - that I am a waste of time. I even felt that from here, life is going to be a lonely road for me.

But then with time, good mentors, a lot of self-help books, and spending time with myself and connecting with my own gut I realized "it's not them who disappoint me – it is ME who disappoints ME."

"Know yourself"– you are your best investment. You are your best support. You are your first love. And you will be there for yourself -even if all will decide to leave.

So friend, my dear friend – VALUE YOURSELF.

Here I am sharing an activity with all of you that will help you to know yourself, the things you like, the thoughts that are affecting you, and the people you want to spend time with.

Start doing this exercise every month on the same date and see the changes you get in yourself. For example,

I like to behave like a child around people I LOVE.

Also, note down the changes you feel on monthly basis.

It is also important to know things you don't like. So here is one for your help.

Yes, it is very important to know both what you like -what you do not like at all.

For example – I like to spend time with people who discuss ideas but I don't like to be around those who only discuss ideas and don't work on them.

As it is written and said, knowing others is WISDOM, but knowing ourselves is ENLIGHTENMENT.

One day, the master was watching a practice session in the courtyard. He realized that the presence of the other students was interfering with the young man's attempts to perfect his technique.

The master could sense the young man's frustration. He went up to the young man and tapped him on his shoulder.

"What's the problem?" he inquired.

"I don't know," said the youth, with a strained expression.

"No matter how much I try, I am unable to execute the moves properly."

"Before you can master the technique, you must understand harmony. Come with me, I will explain," replied the master.

The teacher and student left the building and walked some distance into the woods until they came upon a stream. The master stood silently on the bank for several moments. Then he spoke.

"Look at the stream," he said. "There are rocks in its way. Does it slam into them out of frustration? It simply flows over and around them and moves on! Be like the water and you will know what harmony is."

The young man took the master's advice to heart. Soon, he was barely noticing the other students around him. Nothing could come in his way of executing the most perfect moves.

What are your learnings from the above story?

Share it, and write it on a blank page. Because again remember, "Your learnings can light someone in the darkness, just as this book, the stories, the activities, and the experiences are your light in the area of darkness in your life.

. . . .

. . . .

. . . .

. . . .

. . . .

Now that you have written your learnings from the story, how did that make you feel?

In the above story, we learned about being in a state of flow right? So now the question here is how do we do that?

And that is why as I mentioned we need to understand ourselves, how is it possible for anyone to keep flowing in the right direction if they don't know where to stop and where are they heading.

I am going to repeat here, "know yourself, and understand yourself so that you can value yourself. "

The transition age – ok! So you have spent 5 years on learning, 2-3 on implementing the learnings. Perfect, so now just go and enjoy the transition age. Enjoy the relationships, the job-business, the wealth the health, and all the things you have thought you would be doing in these years or at this age. Go enjoy!

Oh! Why you are not moving? Is there still something that is holding you back? Not letting you enjoy the transition?

The transition should have been easy and fun right?

Is it? Is it not easy?

Now this age is nothing but just a reflection of how were the earlier two phases, and how you have spent them. Imagine, you just have taken 50% of all the learnings that had to be taken during the learning age. And out of that 50%, you were only able to apply 30% of the learnings in your life.

So how will you be able to live about 100% of the transition phase?

Now of course you will ask how would we know this? And the answer here is "NO YOU WON'T". You cannot know everything beforehand, sometimes you can just predict but it won't work for long either. You can only connect the dots once you are done living the moment and start looking at it from a third-person perspective or a broader perspective.

So now again here, if you are not enjoying the transition age that means you left something in the past that you are going to need in the present and the future. Yes, my dear friend, your subconscious will hold you back if you have missed the learnings that you are going to need. It is just like a warning alarm. It is just like the last-minute check you do in any hotel room before checking yourself out.

And I personally feel it is a very good blessing again. So now we get a chance to go back, connect the dots, get the learnings, and come back and re-start.

During my workshops, I do teach NLP exercises to people about how they can just go back in the past, collect the learnings, and come back in the present and re-start where they have left, yes these all are visualization techniques. This kind of exercise helps us to reconnect with ourselves and get our intuition active.

So do try visualisation techniques according to your needs.

I hope you have got an idea of how these three phases are connected to each other and how these three phases are important for our overall progress in every decade.

Some people plan their life in such a way that they tend to miss a lot of things, and a lot of moments, but I believe that if you check your life in this format it can lead you to great transformation.

Note – you will think you know and understand everything in all the three phases, just cut the thought then and there and remember "possibilities over Assumptions. "

So now if you are all set to move one step forward in your life, let's start the journey of experiences, activities, and self-discovery.

Each chapter will be your guiding light,

Each activity will be your friend in need,

Each page will lead you to a new you.

Table of Contents

Mindset

You know, one of the most powerful words I have heard as a teenager was "MINDSET" and I also learned "you are what you think."

I also remember an activity I used to do for self-help purposes. I used to take a day off from my regular life and sit at a place where I used to get peace (it was always a dhabha at Highway), and on a page, I used to encircle my age. After which I used to right my mindset at that particular age about a few important parameters of my life (we all have different). For example, Love, money, family, friends, dreams, bucket list, unfulfilled wishes, my emotional strength, etc.

This activity helped me a lot to be in a state of awareness during those years. Also, it helped me get more connected to myself.

Also, it used to help me to know what drives me?

What has the hold of my energy?

And if I get to know that I am getting driven by my temporary aspects, I used to quit it then and there itself.

Yeah, I know it's a very small activity, but, my dear friend, it can change your MINDSET for better things in life.

So why don't you start this chapter by doing this exercise and start getting connected, because this is not a book you just read and enjoy.

This is a journey you take – improve and enjoy.

I have met a few sixty-year oldies who behave like twelve. Also, I met a few 15s behaving like my grandpa sometimes.

What makes them do this?

Why are they acting like this?

And the answer is very simple, it's not just the number of your age, it's also the mindset you have at that age.

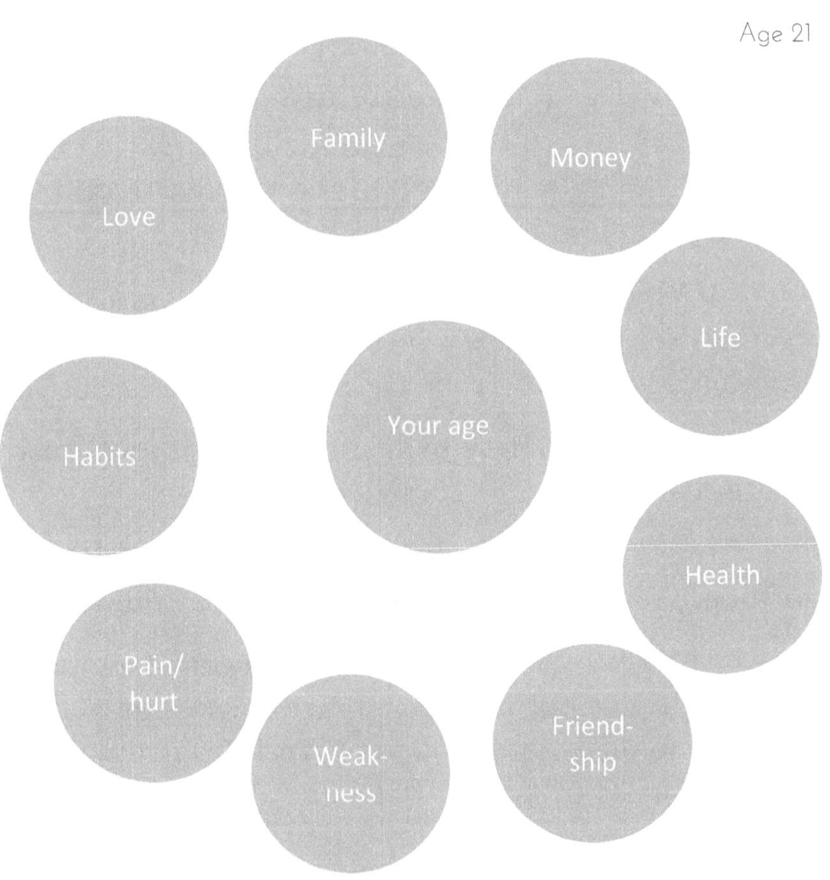

How does this exercise make you feel?

....

....

....

....

I still remember the time, when I used to doubt if I am going to make it? If things will fall in the exact place where I want them to be? Or even sometimes, am I the kind of person who wins?

All these questions have one common thing in them, FEAR. Yes, fear is something that drives you at a speed of more than light. It makes you feel worthless as well as useless at times.

If you are feeling this fear, you are very much normal. Yes, I will repeat it for you "YOU ARE VERY MUCH NORMAL."

Now all you have to do is to get to the root cause of this fear and have to change your mindset.

Age 21 is the age I made the "The Mistakes of fortune." Yes, I have started calling them by this name.

Those were the decisions I made at that moment to actually get out of that moment. Those mistakes have made me what I am today. Yeah, sometimes it's a tour of heaven and at the same time, it's a royal rumble inside.

But don't worry, at the end of the day we all get fine. We all eat, sleep, breathe, and the show will keep running. But here making peace with those mistakes is very important.

Life is not fair or unfair, it's not easy or hard, it is the meant to be, yeah, life is "meant to be."

And I realized it when I started thinking about my life at the very moment when I was writing this chapter.

What would have happened if I had avoided that one decision, or that one friendship, or that business partnership, or that one person I probably loved at that very moment.

What difference it would have made?

People always tend to waste their time on this question. But here the real question you should ask yourself is "am I sure it would have been better than this?"

So now, stop asking and clinging to this very question. Just start and take the first step to connect with yourself and change your mindset wherever needed.

I was 21, I was naive, and I made mistakes. I paid for them, learned from them, left them behind, but made sure to improve & grow.

One sure thing I have learned from the age of 21 is "Once you start growing, those mistakes start turning into a blessing for you."

So yes, I am blessed that I have not avoided that one decision, or that one friendship, or that business partnership, or that one person I probably loved at that very moment.

I am blessed that I lived them, and then only "moved ahead."

Because as I mentioned earlier, life is "Meant to be."

I still totally understand that for you, my friend, it's hard to digest that your mistake can lead you to a fortune. And believe me, I respect that.

But the only question that matters here is "do you respect yourself enough to let this pass & move ahead?"

Answer this as quickly as possible or take as much as time you need.

Meanwhile, I will share with you the first three mistakes that I did till age 21, oh, those mistakes.

Sweet but were bitter to digest at those times, small, really small…but used to look as big as a giant Thanos.

Harmless but a bit scary.

But as I already said, "I am blessed I experienced those mistakes, learned from them, and then moved ahead."

MISTAKE NO. 1

Not unboxing OUR own potential

As a kid we always used to think we are the "HERO", the iron man, superman, or sometimes thor, the one who will fight the villain, or will save the world, and also will make everyone happy, and most importantly, will get love from people we desire.

But in all these filmy scenes, what a majority of people don't recognize is, "We don't need to be the hero."

To enjoy and to get love, "We just need to be we," and keep doing what excites us, what brings a big smile to our faces. We need to just do things that make us feel complete. All at once, we just need to do what we need to do. And the rest will be taken care of by time and the few days, or few months, or few years NEW YOU.

So here I will definitely suggest you, my friend, as you decided to read this book, "do things that your current potential loves to do and then only move towards increasing your potential." Don't rush into improving without enjoying the current potential you carry. So, unbox your potential box, this freaking box is full of great surprises.

MISTAKE NO.2

Trying to understand everything

Oh, this one, I have I'll say I wasted a lot of time, emotions, and sometimes the energy to understand everything which now sometimes I think "kar bhi kya leta samajh ke wo sari chize?' Yes, of course, we, as human beings, have a very powerful ability to feel our emotions, and a lot of time due to emotional flow as I can say, we tend to OVERTHINK, and then you know few dumbasses told me "overthinking is bad." So, I genuinely have a question for you here, Would Graham Bell have invented the telephone with thinking & thinking & thinking and a lot of overthinking about it? Was it possible for Steve Jobs to innovate apple devices without over thinking about it? The answer is a "BIG NO." Because, my friend, overthinking is not at all harmful, it opens up a lot of doors of ideas for you. Whereas I totally suggest that "negative overthinking is harmful to our confidence and self-image. So just be aware of that."

Also, remember a very simple thing "you are human, not google to know everything." And when it comes to understanding, I suggest "don't try to understand everything. It won't help you in the long run, because it will kill your time in what I call "the waste cycle."

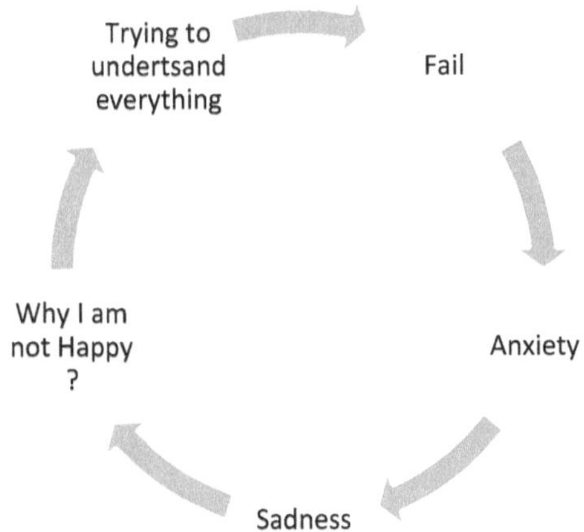

So my friend, oh my dear, my…. Do not try to understand everything. But keep taking action on whatever you have understood and see the doors opening themselves.

MISTAKE NO. 3

Not knowing what to know

Just imagine your favorite car, now imagine taking that car for a drive.

Enjoying?

Now just imagine you have been driving for 14 hours straight, and the worst thing is "you don't know when to stop? Where to stop?"

Even if you know how to stop, if you don't know where and when to stop it will get boring and then frustrating to drive that car even for a minute from then.

But in life, our life we can decide. Right?

But one thing we all miss is, "we ourselves can decide to stop whenever & wherever as per we want."

So now here just imagine planning where to stop?

When do you need to take a break?

When do you need to rest?

If you plan this in a bit advance with an open mind for possibilities, don't you think it will be good for you.

In fact, now do one more thing, imagine you have your favorite person with you on this ride. Now how are you feeling?

Feelings of boredom, or frustration changed?

Exactly at this age, especially from 16 to 19, parents should just help their kids with things they should know during their ride and not focus on "what you should not know/not do?"

Rather parents and mentors should guide them with things they should learn or do in order to get what they want to achieve.

It is very important to know what we should know.

What habit, value, or behaviour, or which person, book, or sport can help us get what we truly desire.

So, my friend, in order to know what you should know I strongly suggest, start spending some time with yourself with just a pen and paper just for 20 minutes a week. The more frequently you do this, the more you will connect with yourself.

I will also share a very easy as well as an effective exercise for you in the next chapter.

These are the first three mistakes we often do during this age, which age?

Oh, some people do it till they die.

As it is said, "some people just tip-top their way to death."

But the moment you decide to learn from these mistakes and then take action and move ahead, you get yourself out of that "Some people" group.

The group that actually succeeds in life.

I remember a participant from one of my workshops, who came to me with a serious depression problem. As she told me "I am always worried, I don't know about what? But I am always worried.

When I asked her when she thinks she has started developing this idea of worrying about things she share a very particular as well as a detailed episode of her life.

This woman, a 56 aged woman was in fact among the very successful people I have met. She started her own textile company with her husband and has done tremendous growth. Even after he passed away at a young age, she kept the dream alive and kept working hard and doing both the roles for her 3 kids. As I said I consider as a successful person, she raised all the 3 kids with good values. But as the kids started growing young she started worrying about their habits, their choices of decisions, their education -career- relationships, and a lot of other stuff that she used to see in their life.

Now what she forgot is she is looking at her kids' life from a third-person perspective but the kids are living it the way they should have lived. They were making some good as well as some poor choices. They were failing at some relationships and losing some money exactly the way teenagers should have done.

Her mistake was not worrying about them, in the end, she was the mother who was trying to do both the roles. Her mistake was, while she was worried about the kids' life – she forget her own. She forgot that even she was supposed to do some mistakes, learn from them, and then implement & grow.

So basically she stopped learning about things she needed to do in her own life and hence she started being worried about failure.

Yes, failure – she was not just worried about the kids, she was worried about their failure. She was so worried about failure that she assumed that if she doesn't look after the kids – they will fail too.

And from here the pattern of worrying started.

It is exactly what happens to a garden when we don't grow the flowers and fruits we want.

What happens there?

All the waste grass still grows, right?

Exactly what happens with our minds, When we don't plough the goals we want to achieve – random goals like depression, anxiety, diseases & anger starts growing.

So here is what we are supposed and start doing is – start thinking about the goals, the relations, and the life we want rather than things we do not want to happen to or with us.

While writing this book do you really think every parameter of my life is balanced?

Everything is going exactly the way I want to be?

My dear friend, you know the answer. But I still, apart from all the factors, have consciously decided to write and complete this book exactly the way I thought, in fact even better.

Because it's not my job to stay away or keep the waste weed away from me, but it is my freaking job to plough and grow the flowers I want to blossom in my garden. And exactly like that, this book is the flower I will love to have in my garden of life.

There will be other issues too. But then this book will keep my life fresh and beautiful.

And in the same way, you should start ploughing, nourishing, and growing the goals and things you want in your life rather than worrying about failure.

Because failure only arrives when we close all the doors of opportunities for us.

I hope you have closed all the doors, I hope you have answered all the questions this chapter had for you, and I genuinely hope you have done the activities this chapter will like you to do.

And lastly, I hope you have also identified the mistakes you have been doing that harmed or troubled your mindset.

If yes, CONGRATULATIONS -now you have made yourself open to learning. Because the 1st step towards LEARNING is ACCEPTING.

If NO, no worries, we have a long journey to be done together, yes, together. Because as I have said earlier, THIS BOOK IS YOUR FRIEND IN NEED, AND A TRUE FRIEND IS ALWAYS THERE BY YOUR SIDE NO MATTER WHAT. I repeat "NO MATTER WHAT. "

Now let's complete this chapter by thanking ourselves that we are capable of identifying our mistakes.

And blessed to take action on them.

I am waiting for you in CHAPTER 2, to talk to you about the "sense of achievement. "

"*Most of them might be thinking that this activity for realising the importance or realising the facts which a human tries to deny or to get to know the importance so that he can work hard and excel but when went into the roots of this activity it's like a tree which has many branches which can lead us to various life aspects.*

For me this activity was a way to find out the real purpose of life. We all know there're are only two crucial days of our life one is the day on which we are born, and the other is when we get to know 'WHY' we are born. If we have the 'why' then all the 'how' turns into illusions which can be breakdown and made again by us in the way, we want.

By this activity I got to know that life of a human is limited but not in terms of time, money, happiness but in the terms of positive thoughts, as this is the only factor which can bring a human life limitless so from now negative thoughts will have a limit and positive thought will be limitless.

After completing the activity under the guidance of Himanshu sir I finally came up to a conclusion"

- **Aum Patil**

Notes:

Sense of Achievement

Ever helped an old person to cross the road?

Or a homeless with an ounce of food?

Or a gym fellow to lift those extra 10?

Ever supported a friend in crisis?

Yes?

No?

With both of the answers, we have a lot to learn.

I today, hear a lot about some kids taking drugs, some sort of addiction or getting too much attached to that one person they know maybe is not a fit for them, or addicted to some mobile porn & sometimes those brainless games they waste their time to.

Apart from feeling pity for them, ever thought about why they do that? Ever tried to talk them out of addiction?

So here is what I observed dealing with people who shared their life journey as well as their stories of "why their life is, what it is? "

So I was having a conversation with a mid-age woman, let's say about 47-48, a talented as well as an honest one. She used to be a teacher and while she was telling about her teaching career, she seems to be joyful. Yes, joyful until she started telling me about her life and how her life took a turn she never thought it would.

Got married at 25, had her 1st kid at 29, and 2nd at 36. Being a teacher before her marriage she was quite underrated. Yes, under-rated. Now of course even you will be having this question "who under-rated her?"

Who under-rated her?

No... Not me, not her family, neither her friends nor the society.........but she did that thing for herself.

Got married, had her first kid.....then her second in 7 years of span.

No, no, no, my friend this was not at all her mistake.

The real mistake here was, that the moment the mother inside her was born, the teacher was left behind.

And baaaaammmm, this is a MISTAKE.

So she made herself totally busy doing all the household chores, the taking care, and growing kid's part.

Did those things what a mother does for her kids. Then she believed or at least thought this is her life now. This is what she is supposed to do for the rest of her life. This will be her success as a person, a wife, and a mother…..

And the passionate teacher left behind. In fact, slowly was passed & dusted.

10 years later from then and then 15 her kids got welcomed into their TEENAGE, and you know how it is right? To be a teenager or have kids who just got hit by puberty. Slowly & then quickly, these kids started spending more time with friends, or at school or at a sports ground, or sometimes what nowadays people call "Alone time." Nope, this is not what we can call a wrongdoing right? So here is what exactly happened for this lady now, for a better part of her life has been spent taking care of her family. And now that family needs their own space.

And now she has all the space she needs right?

But now was it that easy to cope with?

She spent most of her time idle, which leads to thinking, leads to overthinking, and then a lot of times "NEGATIVE THINKING." The time she spent as a teacher always gave her a sense of achievement. The time she took care of and raised her kids gave her a sense of achievement. So what now? What will give her a sense of achievement? This exactly is the feeling of being worthless, useless, and slowly becoming lifeless.

So the word here "SENSE OF ACHIEVEMENT"makes some sense to you?

The lady was not underrated by age, she got under-rated by "HER SENSE OF ACHIEVEMENT. " And I am sure here we meet a lot of people who, unaware of their real sense of achievements, just trying to tip-top their way towards another day. And this slowly become a chain of patterns they tie themselves to.

We all need to have the "Sense of Achievement"to motivate ourselves to get through these tough, sometimes unexpected times. But for some people, if they don't get a real sense of achievement, they start looking out for a false, or temporary sense of achievement. And for each of their action then, are consequences they don't even think about.

Here if a person does not know what gives him/her a real sense of achievement, they, as human beings, keep filling that empty space with a lot of temporary sense of achievement.

1. A compulsory busy schedule:- I had a friend who use to work twice as I worked. Because he used to think that only by keeping himself busy, he will be happy & wealthy?

So did that help him to become happy & wealthy?

Unfortunately NO. His energy and beliefs got drained one day and he quit that job.

But failed to quit that belief "that only by keeping himself busy, he will be happy & wealthy." So this is just a temporary sense of achievement. Hope you didn't fall for this?

Being busy and keeping yourself busy are totally different things, so their results are also totally different. At times people keep themselves busy by going out with friends on a regular basis just because they don't want to face the silence and emptiness of the evening they are experiencing.

Keeping busy to kill the time is just like mixing wheat, grains, and rice together and then separating them, it will keep you busy. But what exactly have you achieved?

So once again I will repeat here, be busy enjoying your life, your age, your year, your month-day, and each second you live by.

Be busy doing things that really give you a sense of achievement but do not just try to keep yourself busy just to kill time.

1. A compulsory relationship:- nowadays there are a few trends or I can say compulsive trends are whooping the market. Of course, 1st is "Entrepreneurship", 2nd is "iPhone" and the 3rd one is "Compulsory Relationship."

Let me tell you a fun fact here. We all work, strive each second, wait for the appraisal, eagerly pray for the promotion, buy a house, get a car, invest in stocks, and do other 145 things to keep ourselves away from stress.

And that itself is a fun fact nowadays because people are stressing out due to workload, some have started to hate each second of their job they are doing. Some are just cursing the house they have got because the EMI"s are big but they feel the house is not. Some are even fighting with siblings for the bigger piece of the stakes and some are literally dying because they think their life has been filled with poverty issues.

So where do all this property, salary, and stocks have led you?

My dear friend, all this of course gives some good meaning to our lives, but relationships -true relationships are the meaning of our life.

But again as people have started getting disconnected from themselves, they have started making or being in a compulsory relationships. A compulsory friend just because you don't want to be alone, a compulsory job because you are shy and have low self-esteem to ask and get what you deserve, a girlfriend or boyfriend because you don't want others to think low of you or that compulsory business partner just because you don't trust yourself that you alone can pull it off.

Now here a lot of people I know have been doing this for a better part of their life and it has been their second nature. You will never find them alone, most of the time they would be spending with people they call friends, and most of the time with other people where they will be talking about their other friends.

And their days are filled with all these things and at the end of the day, they are the people with a lot of friends outside (it at least seems like that). But I personally know a few of this kind and let me tell you, my friend, "it is not working out good for them." It is exactly like running to one thing to get rid of other and then running to another to hide from the one they have started running from. And it becomes a giant wheel that they don't get ready to stop.

Being alone and getting alone are two very different things, my friend, all you need to do is to know where you actually belong and where you are not. But again this will need some "DIYs"and self-identifying. You yourself need to identify what & where you belong and what doesn't add value in your life.

Here, I will leave you to do some thinking. I will come back to you on this again in some other chapter. But here you need to do some thinking on your own. (I hope you remember the DIY age). The more you do it for yourself, the more you will grow.

2. An Addiction- so what was your age you first had a cigarette? What was your age when you had your 1st drink out of depression? What was your age when you found out that you are addicted to the person who has left your life way long back?

Okay wait, I am going to give you a guilt trip for making some choices on your own. We all do it at one point or another.

But let me share an experience with you where I have also learned a lot of things about the human mind and how we should learn a theory which I call "the replacement theory."

Yes, I don't know how and when it came to my mind but I realized we have been doing this when we were kids and we totally forgot this growing up.

So, I met this honest, pretty, and a happy go lucky 18-year-old girl back in 2019. No, it was not a date. It was a serious meeting with her parents where they were complaining, lashing, and sometimes even cursing about their daughter and the way she has been behaving. I knew there is always another side to a story. I felt so bad for her and also wanted to help her. So we started her counselling sessions and decided that we will meet twice a week for the next 7 to 8 weeks.

1st week went well and we started talking. I mean she started talking I merely uttered a word. 2nd week was also good where we, I mean she talked about her life, her college, friends, hobbies, birthdays, the guys she rejected, and also about her crush.

But there is a beautiful thing about the sessions, it takes 2 to 3, sometimes 4 to 5 sessions for people to move from "this is me" to "this is the reason I am like this."

And this journey was very important for the girl. The minute she started explaining the reasons why she is like this and why she does the things she does or why she is "what people are not liking", the first thing we both there realized is that she herself always knew the reason – the problem and the solution. All she needed was a replacement.

A replacement?
What exactly does she need to replace?
What exactly do we need to replace?
And how will we know that are we making the right replacement?

If you are looking out at me for answers, then you need to return to the learning age again.

But if you are ready for some DIYs. This chapter can help you to fill out the missing pieces of the puzzle you are trying to solve.

But first, learn "THE REPLACEMENT RULE. "

This theory, I have made when I was struggling to cope with the emotional baggage I used to carry when I was 20 or 21. This baggage was heavy and also unnecessary. But yet, we humans, carry our past emotional baggage all the time. So now when I was struggling with this baggage and didn't know what to do? How to get out of incidents, rather than accidents that had happened in the past and have no connection to my present or future I took that brave decision of letting this baggage go. "I can do it, I should and I will do it. " I gave it a lot of thought about how I can get rid of the emotional pain of past events that is causing and hurting me in the present.

One day I was just going through some albums from childhood, what a time it was.

We used to ask for chocolate, if not my parents used to give me something similar to it. If I asked for a burger or a Franky wrap, my mom used to give me something similar as well as good for the body. If we asked for money, they gave me the thing or toy or bat that I said I would buy with the money.

Oh! In childhood times, one friend stops talking to us and I used to have others to make me happy. One subject seems to be hard, I used to choose the easy one to cheer myself up. The sport I thought I am weak at, I started playing the one I was good at to keep my self-esteem high.

And at one point or another, we all did it and there is nothing wrong with it. In the end, we need to be happy and feel & have a sense of achievement right?

And what was the harm of this? Nothing right.

So just think about this, we used to keep ourselves secure, happy, motivated, and keep our self-esteem high just by replacing something less important with something that makes more and better impact on our life. Then why don't we do this now? Nowhere in everyday life do we go through something or the other. Life has become somewhat complicated, in fact, so complicated that our one has multiple good as well as the bad impact on our and others' lives too.

So I started doing a regular based activity that I started and kept doing it for around 2 months, to see if it is really possible to replace and let go of things that don't serve growth or happiness in my life. You should also give it a try, my friend, you never know if it can transform your life in a very positive manner.

So let's do one thing, let's keep this book aside for the next 2 days, and just keep doing the exercise and then come back and resume. Do not forget the DIY age, the more we do things for ourselves, the more we grow and develop. And our motto to read this book is to take help and grow. Not just finishing this book and going to the next one.

Take a paper and pen and get ready.

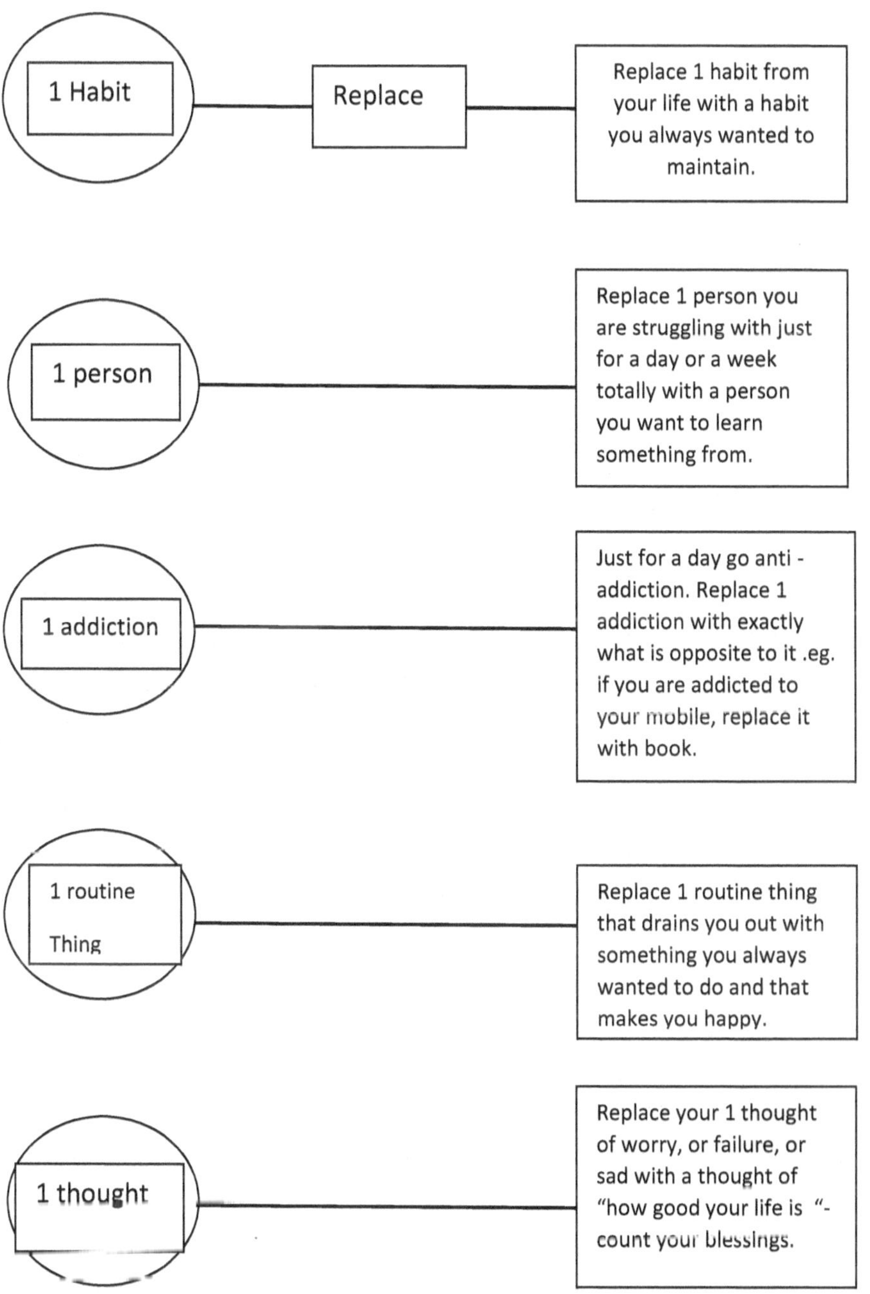

1 Habit
Replace
Replace 1 habit from your life with a habit you always wanted to maintain.
1 person
Replace 1 person you are struggling with just for a day or a week totally with a person you want to learn something from.
1 addiction
Just for a day go anti - addiction. Replace 1 addiction with exactly what is opposite to it .eg. if you are addicted to your mobile, replace it with book.
1 routine Thing
Replace 1 routine thing that drains you out with something you always wanted to do and that makes you happy.
1 thought
Replace your 1 thought of worry, or failure, or sad with a thought of "how good your life is "- count your blessings.

Note – enjoy the process and address the change in feelings while you decide to replace something with another.

I still remember how I replaced going out in the evening just to hang out with a bunch of people that no longer serve towards my growth with going to the gym exactly at that time. You can imagine how useful that would have been.

And then I replaced a lot of things that no longer serve me right. Because in the end, we need to value ourselves even if anyone else is not doing.

I remember one day when I posted a video of me working out in the gym, a close friend of mine teased me about how I am bragging about this gym thing over social media, and the same evening she posted on Instagram her pic with a glass of beer with a caption "it's not bragging when it's BEER."

Of course, I laughed out loud because she failed to understand I preferred the gym over a club or an unnecessary hangout just to avoid loneliness. And if the gym thing is bragging – then for sure the beer thing is.

So the point here is we all brag about a few things, we just need to check what we are bragging about. And we see that few things are not serving our rights or growth or happiness, we replace them. Replace Netflix with a self-help book – replace TV with a journal – replace getting up late with early morning gym – replace small talks with meaningful conversation – replace hiding behind our own shadow with living it out.

Just one right replacement and it can change your life in the right direction. But again don't forget while replacing anything, make sure it gives you the right "sense of achievement."

This activity may not make your life exactly the best in one or two days, but it will definitely make you a better person than you were yesterday.

Share your experience about the activity and then only move ahead to the next.

....
....
....
....
....

I wanna be -_____________________

I really hope you didn't fall for this, but if you have been through any of this or all of them…..

Don't waste much time now.

You just need to know what exactly gives you "THE SENSE OF ACHIEVEMENT?"

As I earlier mentioned in chapter 1, we as human beings need to what exactly we want.

But let me tell you, my dear friend, "you will not know this."

Because with the changing culture & lifestyle, today you want a Ferrari, tomorrow a BMW and on 5ht of march you fall in love with your old bicycle.

You never know. Yes, you never know is the excuse people use to avoid that they have done something wrong or when they want to stall on a decision. But you know, or should know what is it exactly that gives you the real sense of achievement. Or else a lot of people become a "wanna be."

Some colour their hair just to feel stand out from others, ripped jeans, highlights, expensive mobile phones, unnecessary parties to avoid seem to be boring, cool Instagram profiles, and a lot of meaningless shit just to show the world "how happening my life is." But sensible people end up looking "how wanna be I am" and "how wanna be my life is." People who don't know their purpose or what their meaning of being here will always waste time on meaningless conversation, unhelpful rallies, fights, and a lot of things that just give a false sense of achievement.

One of my students when I asked why were you absent yesterday told me, "Sir I was in a political rally." Can you just imagine this? A 16-year-old has gone to a rally by missing his tuition. Is that rally going to serve him right? Is it worth missing his tuition for it?

But yeah let's accept this, he was not an ideal student –in fact, he almost failed in all of the subjects. Not good in sports, not other talents, at least seem to be. So how will he get any of the sense of achievement?

The rallies, the fights, the top to bottom challenges with friends, and a lot of things because nowadays all this is getting normal, in fact, some think this is special.

So it is very important for us, as mentors and guides, to such people to help them understand what exactly is serving them right and what just seems to be right but won't contribute to their growth. While writing this book – I have kept a lot of things aside, networking, parties, mobile phone, something even getting out, and sometimes for days I have not spoken to people other than my family members. Because each word I typed, each activity I shared, and each completing paragraph gave me a real "sense of achievement" and I strongly realized "when I read books, it helped me understand others – but when I am writing this book it helps me understand myself and I am feeling more connected to myself.

So before we move to the next chapter about "THE 3000 breakups" just make sure you have completed this chapter wholeheartedly and not just read it for the sake of finishing it. Remember "DIY." And the more you will do, the more you will grow. So go inside, and know what exactly gives you the sense of achievement.

So here is one helpful, I believe and a quick activity you can run yourself through, just to know what exactly gives you "THE REAL SENSE OF ACHIEVEMENT." At your exact or current AGE.

Now here I am sharing a "VEDIC PERSONALITY TEST" for you. The answers will help you to connect with yourself. So answer each question by your gut and intuition.

1.   Answer the questions as to who you believe you are at the core.

2.   Beyond what friends, family, or society have made you choose.

1 . Which of the following sounds most like what you're about?

a)   Values and wisdom

b)   Integrity and perfection

c)   Work hard play hard

d)   Stability and balance

2. What Role Do You Play In Your Friends Circle/ Family?

a)   I Am Comfortable Dealing With Conflict & Helping People Find Middle Ground. My Role Is The Mediator.

b)   I Make Sure Everything And Everyone Is Taken Care Of. My Role Is The Protector.

c)   I Help My Family Understand Work Ethic, Hustle, And The Value Of Having Resources. My Role Is Material Support.

d)   I Focus On Nurturing And Wanting A Healthy And Content Family. My Role Is Emotional Support.

3. What is most important to you in a partner?

a)   Honest and smart

b)   Strong presence and power

c)   Fun and dynamic

d)   Reliable and respectful

4. What do you watch most often on TV?

a)   Documentaries, biographies, human observations

b)   Entertainment, politics, current affairs

c)   Comedy, sports, drama, motivational stories

d)   Soap operas, reality TV, family, gossip, daytime shows

5. Which best describes how you behave under stress?

a)   Calm, composed, balanced

b)   Irritated, frustrated, angry

c)   Moody, loud, restless

d)   Lazy, depressed, worried

6. What causes you the most pain?

a)   Feeling like I don't live up to my own expectations

b)   The state of the world

c)   A sense of rejection

d)   Feeling disconnected from friends and family

7. What is your favorite way of working?

a)   Alone, but with mentors and guides

b)   In a team as a leader

c)   Independently, but with a strong network

d)   In a team as a member

8. How would your ideal self-spend spare time?

a)   Reading, in deep discussion, and reflecting

b)   Learning about issues and/or attending political events

c)   There are no such things as spare time! Networking, connecting, working

d)   Enjoying time with family and friends

•   9. How would you describe yourself in three words?

a)   Idealistic, introverted, insightful

b)   Driven, dedicated, determined

c)   Passionate, motivated, friendly

d)   Caring, loving, loyal

10. In what type of environment do you work best?

a)   Remote, silent and still, natural

b)   A meeting room or gathering space

c)   Anywhere and everywhere

d)   A space specific to my type of work: home, office, etc.

11. What's your work style?

a)   Slow and reflective

b)   Focused and rushed

c)   Fats and rushed

d)   Specific and deliberate

12. How would you like to make a difference in the world?

a)   Through spreading knowledge

b)   Through politics and activism

c)   Through business and/or leadership

d)   Through local community

13. How do you prepare for a vacation?

a)   By picking my reading materials

b)   By having a focused plan of sites to visit

c)   With a list of best bars, clubs, and restaurants

d)   With an easy-going attitude

14. How do you deal with tough conversations?

a)   Look for a compromise

b)   Fight for the most objective truth

c)   Fight to prove I'm right

d)   Avoid confrontation

15. If someone in your life is having a bad week, what do you do?

a)   Give them advice and guidance

b)   Become protective and encourage them to improve

c)   Urge them to have a drink or take a walk with me

d)   Go to them and keep them company

16. How do you see rejection?

a)   It's a part of life

b)   It's a challenge I can rise to meet

c)   It's frustrating but I'll move on

d)   It's a real setback

17. At an event/party how do you spend your time?

a)   I have a meaningful discussion with one or two people

b)   I usually talk with a group of people

c)   I somehow end up the center of attention

d)   I help with whatever needs to be done

18. How do you feel if you make a mistake?

a)   I feel guilty and ashamed

b)   I have to tell everyone

c)   I want to hide it

d)   I reach out to someone supportive

19. What do you do when you have to make a big decision?

a)   I reflect privately

b)   I ask my mentors and guides

c)   I weigh the pros and cons

d)   I talk to my family and friends

20. Which best describes your daily routine?

a)   It changes moment to moment

b)   It's very focused and organized

c)   I follow the best opportunity that comes up

d)   It's a simple scheduled

I read this question in a book, I don't remember the name but I do remember the message, and it was crystal clear. "Know yourself." Because as it is said, "knowing yourself is the beginning of all the wisdom."

Notes:

41

Glass Half Full

Suddenly one day I got to know that I had a heartbreak.

So one day I woke up normal, I was 20. And I had a breakup (reasons won't matter) hahaha…now it's totally ok to laugh over it.

So anyway, I had a breakup and of course, I was sad & angry and a hundred and twenty-five other things. The other day I started to develop a feeling of losing someone very close to me. And of course, it was my first relationship. So I, as a 20-year-old young boy needed some time to process what has just happened to me. Was it too much to ask? I will definitely say no. So I was processing it with the amount of knowledge and mindfulness I had (yeah I know I had very little of it), but still, I was trying. But the real matter here is no matter how hard I was trying nothing seems to be working for me. I started feeling un-resourceful and I was mad about that. I didn't know about breakups and heartbreak in any of the ways in which events were taking place in my life. I always thought till that time that about my life, I know a lot of things. In fact, when this happened I was sad, but not depressed. I was sad for losing a person I have been with for a long period of time. I was sad because of the memories I was living with. But didn't know that my heart was broken into pieces until a couple of days a very good friend of mine started to you know sympathize with me, tells me everything will be fine, there are a lot of fish in the sea and all and told me, in a fact gave me a shock by telling me, "you had your first heartbreak."

I was standing there listening to the guy telling and asking myself "HEARTBREAK?" "1st heartbreak?"

Now, this was something very much new to me. So he explained to me that as my relationship was over, that girl broke my heart. So now my heart is broken? This question haunted me for days. But what was troubling me was something very different.

How is it even possible to have my 1st heartbreak at 20?

Because I was utterly sad when in 2003 India lost to Australia in the World cup final.

I was so sad when I didn't get the bicycle I wanted in standard 3?

I was damn disappointed when I came 3rd in the school elocution competition, where I really felt I deserved to be the first.

Oh, I was so filled with anger when my best friend shared his tiffin with someone else. Doesn't this get counted as "heartbreak" because I know, my friend, you can connect to this totally. So now why a lot of people were judging me for a relationship that ended? A few were even suggesting to me that love is bad, trusting someone is bad, and caring for someone is bad.

Is it?

Should we, as human beings, should stop playing a game just because we didn't play well.

Or should we stop watching a game because the team we were supporting lost that day? Or should we quit thinking about things we love because we didn't get that cycle or that bat or a toy?

Or should I stop caring just, and just because someone I cared about didn't care about me enough?

I know, my dear friend, you just answered all these questions in your mind for me. which of course should become your reasons to "NOT TO GIVE UP."

I, on one hand, didn't have anyone to teach or explain to me how to handle such situations, you, my champ, have this book. Make it your guide to help you and get rid of this heaviness on your chest of this unspecific word "HEARTBREAK."

Let me tell you about a very important incident in my life that helped me understand a few important feelings of my life like what exactly anger is?

Why do we panic? Or frustrate? Or why do we get aggressive?

Why do we love? & and why do we hate?

We all must have always heard about "the glass is half full." So here is what I will like to share with you, the day the relationship ended it took me 6 months to get over all the incidents and all the trouble I went through. Majorly it was the group of friends I used to hang out with whom I had to suffer a lot. Yes, believe me, it was shocking for me as well as it was also a kind of heartbreak. The people with whom you spend most of the day, fun, parties, and memories are troubling you for something which you are learning to handle for the very first time.

I was not only feeling alone but also the pain inside me was increasing every day. But I don't know how and what I had or kept inside me to say whenever I felt like quitting "today is not the day – today is not the day they will see me sweating." And it used to give me so much power and support that I finally made it through those times on my own and with the support of my family and some very significant people in my life.

"Today is not the day they will see me sweating." You can also make this your POWER STATEMENT. It has helped me a lot.

So coming back to the glass half full, it was during those time when I first heard this when a friend was explaining to me that things happen for a reason, and maybe our glass of relationship got full and there was no more space for new memories so the love spilled out. I was so annoyed at him, but it also made sense to me but in a very opposite manner. Yes, in a totally opposite manner, I realized maybe our glass of relationship got empty. Yes, maybe our glass of relationship got empty as we had nothing more to offer to each other. Just imagine the moment when I realized that the glass of our relationship got empty because we both, no longer serve or offer anything to help each other grow and excel in our life. I was finally out of the rage, the fire that was burning inside me keeping me awake for nights was almost gone. Those feelings of anger, hurt, regret, and complaints, all those, are just a few. I felt they just left my body finally and I was feeling damn light in my head. Because just think about it, if you love someone and they also do then you should be a person who adds value to their life. As it is not just love which carries and makes a relationship successful. I hope you are not fool enough just like me to think that only "LOVE" will help you to become successful in your teenage relationships or for that matter in any of your relationships. It takes love, trust, confidence, empathy, contribution, support, and a lot of things on a regular basis to fill that other half of the glass. It takes efforts from both sides to fill the glass with all these things. And when this thought helped me to release the burden of this heartbreak I was finally ME again. I started meeting with people, I started working on my goals, and I was finally the way I was. But here again, it took me 6 months to realize this. And I may have lost a lot of things – important events in those 6 months that maybe will never come in my life again. And I really don't want you to live with this burden ever. So here in this chapter, I will share a few activities and also a few incidents which helped me get through those times and become emotionally and mentally clear about "what I bring to the table and how I fill the glass?"

Yes, we all should always be a giver first, and as it is said givers gain. What you will give will come back to you in 100s of ways, because what goes around comes around, round and round. Yes, it does come round & round to make us realize that maybe sometimes it's us who are not filling the glass and that's why a friendship or a relationship didn't work. And is it not applicable to every relationship in our life except for our family. Because the moment we stop filling the glass of any relationship, we get the chances of ending or damaging it high. And also on the other hand we should keep in mind that it's not only us who has the responsibility to fill the glass. It's half full for them also, and they should also take efforts from their side. And if not, just ask yourself "if you fill the glass all on your own and it still breaks or gets drained or anything that gets the relationship to an end, will it serve you right. Because you will be out of luck there as you have poured everything you had. The trust, the empathy, the care, the childishness, all those things will get drained and then you run a chance of being a glass.

"TOTALLY EMPTY." Now, don't you think a totally empty glass is not something you will like to be called right? So we have got to remember this that when we are talking about relationships and filling our part and maintaining our energy in a relationship, it is not wrong to expect that the other person also should complete their or at least their efforts should be visible. Because let us face this, I did have met a few friends who said a lot of things and promised a lot of things about how important this friendship or this relationship is for them, but their actions were never towards it. In fact, the moment you will need them like really need them, they disappear. Then they have a 1000s of excuses for why they were not there for you when you needed them the most. Sometimes it works, sometimes it's their so-called dreams, or sometimes their other priorities. And at times they will act up as the victim there. But again don't be confused here, I suggest just taking your half-full glass and saving your energy with them so that you will have your feelings, empathy, confidence, and care with you. Don't be bitter for them, don't waste your time screwing them or fighting with them. I suggest just moving ahead, you still have your full glass and I am sure somebody -someday will be totally ready and happy to fill their part without you begging for any of their time or efforts.

I, whenever meet teenagers with a breakup or heartbreak problem, I observed that the person who gave their more than 100% is the one who ends up being a mess if and when the relationship ends. And of course, I have learned it from my relationships with my friends and some of my relationships where I literally gave everything I had to offer as a partner, but I guess it was never enough because it will be you who is filling that glass, so when the relationship or friendship or a business partnership ends you are the one who will lose control of life, they will "MOVE ON" (as one of my girlfriend always told me that we should move on now). They will move on and they will never look back because they have still got their half full of glass. On the other hand, you are just standing stuck in your life with an empty glass, and my dear friend, you tend to suffer in such cases. You will lose confidence, faith, and magic, and sometimes that soft heart of yours will move towards being cold.

But again "it will only matter for you" as it is you standing stuck with a glass empty.

As I mentioned earlier in chapter 1, "life is not easy nor hard, life is not fair but neither unfair – LIFE IS JUST MEANT TO BE." So now here you, yes you, my friend, need to ask yourself a question and when I say a question, this question can only change your life if you honestly follow the answer which you get from your intuition. If you don't follow the answer and don't take the necessary steps or actions to get out of this stuck state, then it is your fault. Because remember one thing, "being broke is not your mistake, but staying broke is."

So if life is just meant to be, is your life meant to be empty? Stuck?

Now I know your subconscious mind has already given you an answer. So are you waiting for some bell to ring here? Just go ahead and start filling your glass on your own to move forward from this stuck state. and remember one thing, "it's your glass, and it's your freaking responsibility to fill it so that yes someday someone will be more than happy to take the efforts of filling the other half and make you complete."

Here now I am sharing an activity with you to help you fill your glass with confidence, love, empathy, awareness, and stop you from self-criticism, and help you to MOVE FORWARD rather than just move on.

While doing this exercise just keep in mind that you are doing this exercise for yourself and keep doing it till you get the answer, "how and what helps you to fill your glass in a very meaningful way."

Let's start filling your glass.

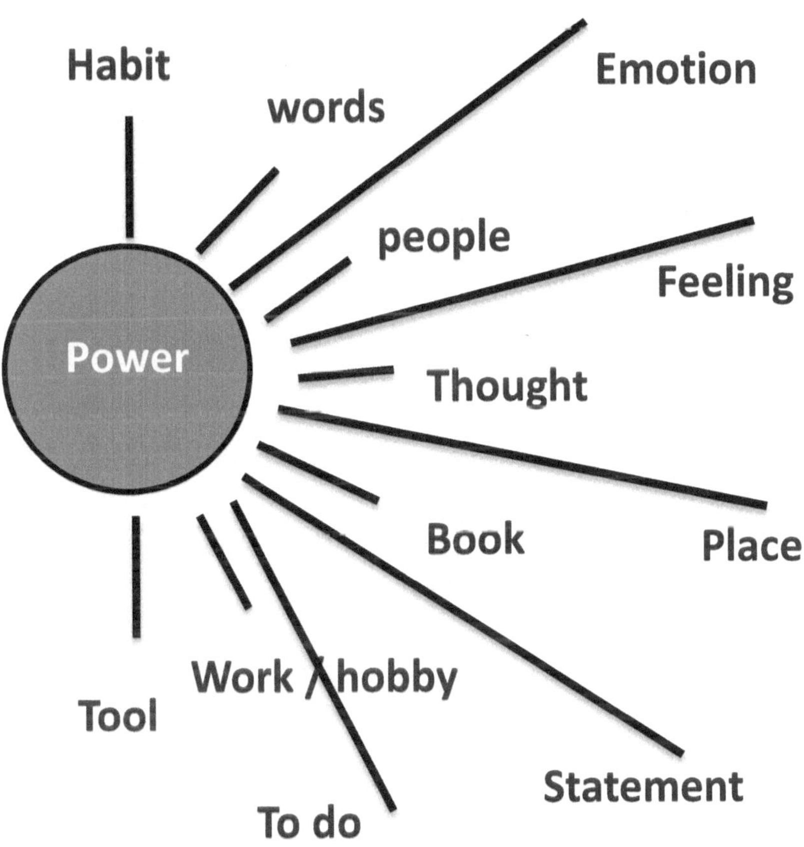

> **I'd rather change it, than stay like it.**
>
> **I'd rather stay, than a change like it.**

How would you know that the things you are filling in to make the glass at least half full are the right ingredients for your success or a relationship to be precise?

So to help you to give your best, and to know what are the right ingredients, the above activity will help you to get your answers, and also will introduce you to your POWER.

While writing this chapter for you, I have spent a lot of time in the "Memory lane of the PAST CITY" to get the right reference as I still remember those times and those feelings of helplessness to filling the glass. It was a road I never thought I would reach the end too. It was a time when wandering around and searching for my own happiness and POWER seemed to be a never-ending job. Restless days, sleepless nights, and the feeling of unresourcefulness became my partners. Yes, I know they were toxic, but I know this now. During those times as I said, all this used to seem like a never-ending part of life. I, in fact, have somewhat accepted that this is how it is going to be. But as I mentioned above, "I'd rather change it, than stay like it or I'd rather stay, than change like it."

And my dear friend, I decided to CHANGE.

Because I always believed if the change is only CONSTANT, so will I be. I really hope this chapter will help you to know your power and also help you to keep your glass ALWAYS HALF FULL.

Now before you move ahead towards the next chapter I will like to tell you the 2 mistakes I have made while trying to keep the glass half full after it used to get drained. These mistakes also helped me afterward and also still doing their things now and then but during those times it was a LOT TO TAKE. At least for me.

1. People will understand you – Now, if you are expecting this blindly, welcome to the city of illusion, my friend. Here you will meet a lot of people who will say, "oh! I understand you, I feel you, I am there for you. But you know the majority of times what happens. And it is not totally their mistake in this. They do believe that they will understand you, or they will be there when you will need them. But here all we need to understand is the way our life is taking a lot of turns and sometimes misfortunes happen. In the same way, their life is also taking some way or other a lot of turns and for you, your turn is difficult and for them theirs is. So expecting that people will understand you will lead you to a bucket full of disappointments and

there are very strong chances that you will fill your glass with feelings of bitterness. Do you wish to fill your part of the glass with feelings of bitterness? If your answer is no, here you have got to remember 1 very important thing for yourself. "Trust everyone – but don't depend on anyone.: Yes, trust everyone that's not an issue at all. Of course, we cannot roam around being skeptical about people and their intentions. We have got to trust people, otherwise, we will become a glass full of doubt, questions, and fear, and most importantly, we won't be able to build meaningful relationships because trust will always be missing in it. And just imagine a relationship without trust, what kind of relationship will it be?

So we, as human beings, should trust people on how they are showing it to us, but that's just their way to portray how they think they are. And I suggest believing them on it. But the real key here is don't depend on them. Nowadays people tend to depend on others without trusting them. Even if the trust part is missing, the relationship seems to work because some way or another, they are dependent on the other one. But is it really a meaningful relationship? Because one day the dependency will end and this is the reason nowadays some people move on from you to someone else. No, it's nothing like that they are better than you or there is nothing to compare. It is just that now that their dependency on you is transferred to someone else. It is how it is, so if something just like this happened to you, my friend, thank God that it saved you, because you cannot make such people happy ever. And you will always keep thinking that you are not good enough. So again you have got to remember this, "it's not necessary that people will understand you, a lot of times they won't. You have got to deal with it, and the best way to deal with it is to "no dependency" even if they leave you tomorrow, your glass should not get drained. So, "no dependency – only trust people." The only person you will be dependent on here is yourself, remember it's your life and it is "DIY- do it yourself." And when you will start trusting people without depending on them, you are the one with no hidden agendas. So you keep the relationship pure. Now even if one day these people break it, you don't lose them – they lose you. And your glass will be safe.

2.   Do not crave attention – hey you, yes you STUPID FELLOW. And here I got your attention. The moment I called you stupid, I got your attention. Even if it is with the feeling of shock or anger, I still got it. Just imagine it is this easy to get someone's attention. Here you really think getting this kind of attention is even important? A lot of people nowadays, especially students I meet and address have an issue of AD

– "attention deficiency" yes, they always crave attention and they will never get enough of it. When you crave attention you start filling your glass with the feelings of FOMO -fear of missing out and again ask this to yourself – are these feelings of FOMO helping you to grow? Because right behind FOMO are hiding the "THEY SAID THIS & THAT people" and these two feelings have a strong capability to keep you awake for nights.

And in the end, we are here to express and not impress. So once you get the habit of craving attention, you try to impress others, and then you tend to become a puppet who does anything to get it.

Teenagers nowadays suffer a lot due to AD. And adults are also not much behind it. To impress others is also an addiction, my friend, make sure you don't fall in for that.

There is a difference between trust and dependency, expressing and trying to impress people. And we, as we grow up, if don't learn the difference, WE SUFFER.

So now I am going to complete this chapter here, but for you, I will draw out one more exercise so that you can help yourself with some sort of understanding of these words in your life.

Words like (trust, dependency, impress, express, FOMO, relationship, and glass half full).

Note – move to the next chapter only after completing this exercise. Do not forget "it's your life, and it is a "DIY."

Understanding your relations

1. Name 10 people who you trust with all your heart, but are not dependent on.

    (1)____________________________

    (2)____________________________

    (3)____________________________

    (4)____________________________

    (5)____________________________

    (6)____________________________

    (7)____________________________

    (8)____________________________

    (9)____________________________

    (10)____________________________

2. Name 5 people you do not trust but still are dependent on. (also, you can jot down the reasons for not trusting them)

    (1)____________________________

    (2)____________________________

    (3)____________________________

    (4)____________________________

    (5)____________________________

3. Write down the name of people with whom you feel relaxed and are able to express the way you want without fearing them judging you.

    (1)_______________________________
    (2)_______________________________
    (3)_______________________________
    (4)_______________________________
    (5)_______________________________

4. People you think drain your glass and do not contribute in you growth.

    ____
    ____
    ____
    ____
    ____
    ____
    ____
    _______________________________.

5. People, you think judge you for being you.

    ____
    ____
    ____
    ____
    ____

____

____

_______________.

6. Express your relationship with the following people and check how you both help each other with the glass.

- Father
- Mother
- Siblings
- Friends (you can name and write)
- A teacher
- A relative
- A mentor

Name these people in your life and express the feelings you get on a blank paper.

Remember, my friend, you should know how to keep your glass full. You can only give if you have enough to give. You can only spread the love if you have it, you can only help others if you are ready to help yourself. You can only spread positivity if you have it in your glass.

So fill your glass with meaningful things. This is the only thing you have.

Enjoy.

How do this chapter and exercises help you?

____

____

____

____

____

____

____

____

____

____

____

____

____

____

_______________________________________.

Hello everyone.
I am here to share my experience which I got after doing the activity given by Sir.

So basically, the activity was to decide what are our main ~~priority~~ priorities in our day to day lives. or what should be the first thing to do when we are confused or with whom we should spend our precious time.

The main purpose behind this activity was to give equal amount of time and attention to that work, to that person, to that place or to that book.

For me, it helped me to arrange my day, the whole time in such a way that made me happy. I was able to give time to my mom and dad, I was able to study properly. was able to cope up with the bad day. I was even able to give time to my hobbies.

Earlier I was not able to get enough time to anything but after doing this ~~aciti~~ activity, I just removed the things from my list which had the least priority or didn't ~~m~~ needed my time.

Thank you so much Himanshu sir for giving me this opportunity and helping me out.

- Tanishka Thakur

Notes:

62

Chapter 4

Success is not the key, the key is Success

During the 18th century, humans used to have a simple and stress-free life. They used to cultivate their own food, and barter for what they didn't have. So not much money involved, you help me -I help you was the culture. The oldest member of the family used to make some rules which everyone else used to follow. Grandfather-father-son all used to farm and help each other survive all the time.

So that was the time of survival of mankind.

Then came industrialization, the Britishers realized that the culture and simplicity of our household is a bit strong to break down, so they came up with a divide and rule strategy. Now to divide a household, color, or gender was not going to work. So they introduced a word for us-SUCCESS, the word which still till date has various meanings and not a single one of them is very much clear. Some are in fact just an illusion of our minds. Some think greed is success, some think a big car or a big house is success, and some think their bank account will tell their success saga. Yeah so coming back to the word, they started putting materializing greed between the young members of the family and introduced them to the word SUCCESS.

If to date just imagine what and how we define this word we will realize that many times we don't even know how or when we will ourselves a successful person. In fact, write it for yourself and check how much we have to think. How much confusion does it create?

What does success mean to you?

____

____

____

____

____

_____________________ .

Today we judge each other including ourselves also in this manner. If you are wearing an "X" brand shirt then only you seem to get called as successful. Your car, house, shoes, bag, watch, mobile phones, and 179 other materials decide if you are successful. But if we go this way this means only rich people are successful. So then all of the others are not. So if we say only rich people are successful, how will we know how much money should we earn to be enough to get called rich. And how will I know that I am rich now and who will provide me a valid certificate? And if only the rich will be known as successful then what the others will get called?

Unsuccessful?

Yes? No?

What is your say on this?

How do you measure if you are successful or rich? Or how do you know someone else is or is not?

When I was in school I always wanted to become the class monitor, that time for me maybe it was success, and eventually, I became the class monitor. During childhood, I wanted to become the captain of our school team, and again I got it. I wanted an expensive mobile phone when I was 20 & I got one for myself. I thought a bike, a house, a phone, a team to handle, and of course, the bank messages, will definitely tell my success story to everyone. But I don't know why even after getting all these things and achieving a few that I have planned and promised myself, I didn't feel or get called as successful. I strived for it, worked really hard, sacrificed a few things I loved, cried alone when things went haywire, and stressed out things that seemed to get out of my control. But success? I don't know where it was? In fact, I doubt it was ever there. So I stopped stressing out about it. No, I don't give up, but for the first time, I realized all this time I was chasing something which was and is already mine. Not just me, but we all.

Yes, my dear friend, success was, is, and always be there at our side. The only and the biggest mistake we do is judge an elephant by its ability to swim. We decide if a monkey is successful if he can fly. And then we judge our success by someone else's definition of it. And then, of course, we tend to fail. And we will frustrate over it. My dear friend, a lot of entrepreneurs have come and a lot of them decided to quit. A lot wake up with a dream but sleep with failure in their hands. Because many times we start chasing success which we don't even know what and how it is? So I realized that we all always have success, and success is not the key here – the "KEY" itself is the success.

So here in this chapter, we will discuss and find out our ways and mindset for this word. Also, we will be discussing a few "KEYs" of your life. I remember my mentor always used to tell me that "either we grow or we decay – and during all those times when we are not growing we tend to decay." What a wonderful idea he sowed in my mind. But I have a question here, "How will we ever know that are we growing in our life or decaying?" How will I know that I am not on a path of growth? Because just imagine if one day when you will wake up thinking that yes I have achieved all the things -you wanted to achieve. But then you get to know that during all this time you were on a path of decay. So we should know that are we growing or we are going fussssssshhhhhh!!!

So here are the 5 pillars in our life that decide what is or will be the quality of your life. Will you live as a victor or a victim – a winner or a loser – a happy person or a stressed one.

And the 5 pillars are,

1. Our health – the topmost priority and the most important pillar of our life is our health. If we have good health, we want to enjoy life, get a new house, buy that luxurious car you always dreamt about, help people, and enjoy each second of life. But unfortunately, if your health is no good and you are struggling with it, all that money, house, relations, car, and a lot of dreams are just left behind. A lot of money, emotions, and energy get wasted. So the next time you will feel you are healthy "consider yourself richer than half of the world's population." I don't mean here that only this will keep you happy or this is "THE ANSWER."

2. Our relations/social image – Aristotle said, "human being is a social animal." And as human beings, we all want and need that people should like us, love us, and respect us. We want to enjoy relationships and we also want to help others. Then why nowadays there is not much mess around us in relationships. May it be any relationship. We, as human beings, are designed

to enjoy other people's company. Then why nowadays do we tend to "go solo." Why do a lot of people feel lonely even being in their own home around their own people? Isn't our home supposed to be the safest place for us? This all is because nowadays a lot of time we judge our relations by materials aspects. Don't you think relationships are meant to be emotional and not logical or based on conditions? I know a few will disagree with this idea, but doesn't it happen with every idea that we have two teams. One supports the idea and the other goes against it. So, I still believe that the moment a relationship becomes logical, it's a win-lose or a lose-lose. And there are a lot of chances of it ending by hurting a lot of people. Again I won't say sorting your relations will be the only "ANSWER."

3. Our financial standing – this is not the most important – but it is something that will ease all the other parameters. As I read it somewhere "if we all are meant to cry – it's always ok to cry in a Ferrari." But the real question here is, "does it really matter if we are not ok? Not fine? Struggling? Will a Ferrari change everything?

Imagine having a breakup on the day you get a promotion.

Imagine you are having a severe headache while driving your favorite car.

Going shopping while you have a deadline to complete.

Or imagine you want to celebrate your so-called "success" and you have no one to celebrate with.

Are you OK now?

But again, of course, this parameter eases the other. If we want to get a car, more money= nicer car. You want to go on a date, more money= nicer date.

We get all, more money = nicer hospital. And a lot of other things.

So again let's not keep any misconception about money, money is good. And we all want good money because, my friend, we all deserve it. But again, I won't say this will solve all of your problems. Think about it. So even this is not "THE ANSWER."

4. Our emotional health- a lot of our lives, a few events or incidents happen that we don't want to happen. But they do, and then we still have to cope with it and keep moving forward in our life because as it is said, "the show must go on." And the show will. So we have to cope with it and get ourselves up all the time. I, while writing this book, thought many times of "not to do this." And believe me, I had 100s of reasons for it, lack of time, lack of funds, lack of ideas, and sometimes lack of motivation. But I still did, you know why – in fact, there is just one reason "I believe it will help me to grow," I realized that we, human beings, are born with 100% emotional strength and so no matter what

we can get it back anytime. All we have to do is to decide and then "DIY." A few will always be there for you, a few will leave, a few will try to get you down, and a few will just stare at you while you do your life yourself. And, my friend, it is totally ok. In fact, it is meant that way. I don't know about you, but I always felt that a few obstacles were meant for me to solve. A few issues in my life occurred just so that I can solve them and get the courage from them to solve the new ones.

I always believed "I am chosen" and I also strongly believe "you are too"-after all, we are gods favorite children. He will never drop us down. So here the question is, do we want to make ourselves emotionally strong?

At the end of the chapter, I will share a wonderful activity for you to know what makes you emotionally strong and where you are draining them.

But don't fall for the thing that only this is "the answer."

5. Our self-image – remember when we used to be kids and our parents used to dress us for a function or a party? Remember? Whenever I try to remember the way they used to dress me up I don't know why but I laugh, and I laugh a lot about this. It's like mom what did you even think while dressing me up like that. How funny and weird I must be looking. But you know what, mom never gets embarrassed about

my question. She just always says, "You looked more than like a hero." And that's it. This is how I learned about self-image. No matter what others are thinking or saying about you until you have your self-image clear and good. Nowadays even our phones have Photoshop which can edit any picture into a masterpiece. And who made this phone, of course, human's right. And I am 100% sure you agree that humans will be always smarter than any of the devices. But as I said earlier we need to believe that we can change our self-image, our financial condition, our relationships, and our emotional strength. As it is said, "if you think you can or you cannot do something, in both the cases my friend -you are right."

While writing this book, in fact, even before I started the 1st chapter, I don't know how many have believed that I will complete it. I don't know how many are thinking that maybe someone will read this book and can start helping themselves. I really don't know if anyone believed that I will be able to think and write a book that consists of almost 25 to 30k words. But, my friend, I did. I knew that once I start, I won't look back and that I won't even call confidence or trust, it is just my self-image that I do believe that this book and the activities will help you to get more clear and a much better self-image. And once the self-image is clear and supports your goals, then you don't stop even if no one believes you.

So you know maybe locking yourself for 1 hour in your room, clean it, arrange it, organize it or mess with it. But make sure that you get a self-image that supports your goal. Because if you don't put a better self-image in your mind, someone else will and then you will have to live with it. Remember 1 thing my friend, "it is called SELF-IMAGE, not HE/SHE gave me this SELF IMAGE." It is a "DIY" thing.

So coming back to the word SUCCESS, I don't think there is just one SUCCESS, just one answer to all our questions.

In fact, my friend, I don't think there is any "ANSWER."

I didn't think only 1 parameter will make us successful. I really don't think or believe when someone says, "SUCCESS IS THE KEY" in fact, as I have written earlier, "the key is the success."

So we need to find our key or maybe "keys" to strengthen and enjoy these 5 parameters and more if you have any. We need to get the key that will let us know "HOW SUCCESSFUL WE CAN BECOME." And as success is already ours how we can maximize it in all of our parameters.

Just stand in front of a mirror and imagine yourself living a healthy and long life where you make a lot of friends and help a lot of people, imagine yourself as a person who is emotionally strong and knows how to enjoy your wealth. What kind of clothes you are wearing?

What kind of people you are talking you?

What kind of food you are eating?

What kind of ideas you are sharing?

What kind of people are your followers? And what kind of people do you follow?

What are those things that will help you to find these keys?

All these questions deserve your answers and you deserve to implement and enjoy all these answers while getting your self-image better and better each day. Wake up, my friend, imagine this book, this chapter, this paragraph, and this very line as your alarm to get up and – find that key.

Do not run behind success just because you read about it somewhere or worst just because someone else read it somewhere and rooted it in your mind, don't chase it just because it is shown in some movie. Our life doesn't have a director to decide if "this is our best shot" if you didn't like it and didn't make growth in this take. Get ready for a new take, just this time with a better self-image and you will see the results. All the shots are the good ones, we just deserve better and hence we just need to get ready for the next shot.

Today when I check my mistakes and the consequences I have faced in the past just because of low self-esteem and a poor self-image, I really hope you don't get to face it. A lot of times someone else got something I thought I deserved just because they have had a better self-image than mine may be or they were emotionally strong that day.

Remember, no matter how old M.S DHONI gets you will face fear if you are bowling him the last over and need to defend 16 runs. No matter how old Ronaldo or Messi gets, if they are shooting a ball towards you and you need to save the goal to win – you will face pressure. That's the kind of image they have in our minds. So here it proves that our mind can even make someone else's image strong by going to their past victories and achievements. So why don't we do this for ourselves?

Because my friend some keys are also hidden in past and you have to face the trouble of past memories and burdens for some time to get to the KEY. I know the past suffering can be hurtful but in the end, the reward will be the key, and it is our past and we don't need to run from it.

I have had people who you know maybe didn't like me, or my work style, or maybe more 365 things about me. Some threw the stones of failure, some may be broke my trust -or worst that some never really care, or someone who really took me for granted, some didn't fight for me, and some didn't take a stand for me when I tried my level best. Yes, I know even you resonate with it and, my friend, I do agree that it is so painful and an energy drainer. I do understand that it takes time to get out of the feeling of losing it all. Sometimes even the self-image is shattered and we start wandering around the city of loneliness. But again even this time is "DIY" and it's us who have to get ourselves out of this stuck, useless phase. And here our self-image has the major work to do. So the next time someone breaks you or you feel hurt for something, just ask these five questions and you will be able to save your self-image for your betterment.

1. Is it going to last forever?
2. Didn't I gain something from it?
3. What are my positive gains?
4. What could this time teach me to become better?
5. How should I move one step forward through it?

I remember in a session, one of my participants started crying while sharing his goals. He was 43 and divorced and had 2 kids. All he was doing was trying to become a good father and give his kids a happy and safe life. As he was 43 and was feeling lonely in his life he was getting anxiety issues and also sometimes he felt he is losing it.

I understand and I know how hard it is to just imagine our life without the people we love. And so I asked him to answer these 5 questions for continuous 7 days. As he completed 7 days, he called me and also sent me all the written things he did for 7 days. He was sounding relieved and may be a bit lighter as he said. When I asked him how was your experience, the most important he told me is, "all my answers got different and I realized I was not suffering because of loneliness, I was depressed thinking about loneliness and how my life will be. But when he answered and he got all his answers different he got to realize that we make our state (mood) all on our own and some past version of that memory has even stopped hurting us, it's the present and future version of that memory and event we make in our mind is what hurts us. And we fail to win through it because how can you win something that doesn't even exist. So, my friend, a lot of people try to forget the past and its memories. That business, that failure, that breakup is not what is hurting you now, it's the present and future memory and consequences that hurt us. So here I will just tell you 1 thing that I used for myself and, my friend, it did work, and then it worked for more people.

Erase the present and future version of that memory and spend some time with the past and real one. And then answer the 5 questions whenever you are ready.

God "why me?" will never come out of your mouth from here on.

For all those years I thought once I solve this, once I pay this debt, once I get out of this heartbreak, once I feel this way. I will start living. Just once these obstacles get vanished – I will finally live my life. But connecting with myself now I realize "THOSE OBSTACLES ARE MY LIFE."

Each day you wake up trying to become successful, each day to realize it will take more time for you to get it, and each day you sleep disappointed. So "SUCCESS MY DEAR FRIEND -IS NOT THE KEY."

So change this pattern from this day and go ahead in your life in the search of the key – or the keys. You will get some – or else at least you will make some. But the moment you will have the KEY. My dear friend, you will be able to open the doors of happiness and satisfaction.

Here are the 7 keys you should start searching for:-

1. What do you think adds value to your life?
2. Which are the things you really want to do in your life even if no one is watching or going to like it?
3. What are the feelings you feel on regular days? What do you think will rescue you from it?
4. Who are those you feel really connected with?
5. How do you think you can add value to others' life?
6. Where or with whom do you feel now you don't need any other answers because they are the answer?
7. Where do you see your life will take you if you make proper use of even these hard times?

These are the keys that will open a thousand doors for you. You can select any one where you feel you will give your best take-but remember, "if not this then that- and if not that then this." And no matter what, we all will get our best take and we are all succeeding.

So, my friend, my dear friend – live, live it like your best shot.

Notes:

79

Losing some battles but winning the WAR

Not so in love with my studies during the school and college times, I grew up playing cricket and it was my "first love." Nothing mattered, summer, winter, rain, exams, fever, or anything when it came to going outside and playing cricket. I was just 8 when I was madly in love with the game. It was always Sourav Ganguly (our very OWN DADA) who inspired me for the game. I remember crying when he got out at 24 during the world cup in the 10th over to Brett Lee, and I kept crying when India lost to the mighty Australians. And as a kid, it was very hard to digest that loss. I am sure the team and the whole nation must have been greaving. But for me that day, my tears meant everything and I don't know how but progressing in my life, I promised myself, the feeling I had that day – I will never let that happen to myself ever again. It is this day when I realize it was that moment when I took the first bullet of disappointment to my heart. I am not much of a person who is able to showcase all my emotions, but it was a feeling I still am not able to hide.

So now I realize when I connect the dots that being a DADA fan from the age of 7 or 8 had made me naturally aggressive in my game of cricket and in my life also. So whatever I did in my life to date, I always choose to be aggressive. It has its own pros & cons but in the end, it was always that way.

So coming back to that feeling, and the promise of never letting this feeling ever bother you again – life sometimes does hit you with a brick on your head. And you don't know how to fight with life – so you swallow your pride and keep your head down. I realized we take a lot of bullets in our life - but only those that beat us which we take directly to our heart. For an instance, the 2003 loss. I understand we are Indians and our biggest tool is our emotions, but as it is said there are always 2 sides to every coin. I realized that I try to run from those feelings - the more I kept experiencing them even during my childhood days. During my 5th standard school game, we lost a final match by 7 runs and that loss blew me off, I didn't eat properly for 4 days – I was having trouble sleeping and was cranky during school hours and at home. It was really hard for me to digest that loss – that bullet hit me deeply into my heart. And, my friend, I didn't like that feeling. Again that day I made a promise to myself, "I will never let myself feel this way ever again."

I will admit that I started running from that feeling – the feeling of losing, the feeling of something very important left behind, the feeling of not getting something that you really prayed for. And I know even you agree with this – this hurts. Right?

I grew up, I kept playing cricket. Winning and losing became a part of the game – and of course, at that time this game was life. So a lot of bullets came, a few I was able to dodge- a few got me hurt. But it is the game and these never-ending bullets gave me a very important message -as I also learned from a video of Mrs. Sudha Murty in an interview, "So what if I lost the battle -I lived the war." And this message was very much clear to me, no matter how many bullets go through me, I won't leave the battle till I win the war. And I believe and have total faith, my friend, the moment you decide not to leave the battle because of some bullets that hurt you, drain you, get the better of you during days or sometimes for daaaaaaays – you win the war.

Today we live in the era of technology, science, medical miracles, touchscreens, automatic vehicles, and whatnot. But the bullets - the bullets are still the same. Today we counsel kids of age 15 or 17 and sometimes adults of 35 or 40's. I realize the bullets are still the same. Not just me, but we have a lot of people who start running with some or the other feelings which they never want to feel again. But this running and this habit of keeping yourself away from this feeling always attract it even if you don't do anything. I realized this the day when I took this girl to meet my parents and they liked her, yeah, my parents have been always supportive and they have done everything which was possible for them in every way. So I took her to meet my parents and they supported it. But in a very few days, came a bullet -the bullet of disappointment. This bullet made me feel like I failed them, I failed them big time. I don't know what mistake I made, what is that I did wrong. But I felt responsible for it -not totally but yeah, I felt I have failed them and this bullet gave me the pain which I have promised I will never let myself go through. But again you lose some battles even if you did everything right. But what matters here is, "don't leave the battle until you get the WAR attitude." Don't start running from the feeling that bothers you – in fact, embrace them, they will cause you pain for a while – in fact, sometimes the pain will feel as unbearable. But you don't lose until you don't decide to leave.

So here, my friend, in this chapter the first thing I will share with you is don't run – don't run from the feeling or feelings just because the bullet has hit hard. Live with those feelings for a while – introspect yourself, check and take the learnings, relive the happy moments even if you know they won't come back, and cry over the loss. But deny leaving. Don't run from your feelings. As I mentioned, these feelings are like bullets – bullets that will follow you wherever you go.

With each day of your life - the more you will survive these bullets, the more you will move forward in your life. The bullets will hit you, hurt you, and make you sad – but keep choosing to stay in the war even after you will sometimes feel that it is over for you.

As it is said, "it's not over until I am breathing." So face these bullets, survive, and get out as a victor from every battle. I remember a dialogue or you can say a self-motivation I used to use when I used to get hit by such strong bullets which I directly took to heart, "today is not the day I will let them see me sweating." And I decided to stay.

So mark all the feelings which you were running from. The more you will write - the more you will be able to face them. (Now this chapter may take you a few days to complete) but believe me, my friend, I am not the same kid who cried over the feeling of losing the WORLD cup. Because I stopped running.

Are you running from any feelings?

____

____

____

_______________________________.

If yes, then write down all the feelings of your experience.

____

____

____

____

_______________________.

Also, what made you feel like it?

____

____

____

____

____

_______.

How do you think you responded?

____

____

____

____

____

As it is always said, it's not the problem that troubles you, but it's your response to it. My response to the 2003 loss was that I took it to heart and then I cried. I think I regretted it and hence that promise came into the scene. So what actually hurt me? The loss? The response? Or the promise?

Because when today we lose, I don't cry, I don't respond in the way I did that time. But the real thing here is that feeling and promise were not only limited to the game of cricket. It is also reflected in my personal and professional life. As I made the promise to myself that I will never let myself feel like this again. I meant I will never feel disappointed, I will never let myself hurt, and I will never lose anything that I love. I will never lose. But even you know, my friend, we have to deal with all this eventually, and so did I. I felt disappointed in a few people, people who I thought were very close to me but eventually, they did or said something that came towards me like a bullet of disappointment. I got hurt by the people I trusted the most. A few cheated, a few left without even giving me reasons, a few treated me as if I am not worth it, and a few didn't fight for being with me. And, my friend, in the end, we are all humans, and in that, I am a naïve one. So yeah, I felt hurt. And this bullet - the bullet of hurt hits hard and straight to the heart and mind. I lost a few things that were very much close to my heart, a few people I never wanted to lose, and a few opportunities I didn't want to slip from my hands, but they did.

This bullet – takes away your confidence for a long period of time. And to get back that confidence, we again need to go to the learning age and the "DIY" age. So all you can do here is 1st identify these 3 bullets and their effects on you and then try not to run from them but try to learn and make peace with them. I know what I am asking here is way more difficult to do than to write. But again my friend, we don't want to leave the war over some lost battles.

Write down things, people, and situations that you feel disappointed with.

____

____

____

____

____

____

_____________________________________.

Write down things, people, and situations that you feel hurt you.

____

____

____

____

____

____

______________________________.

Write about the things, people, and opportunities that you loved and lost.

____

____

____

____

____

___________________.

Not just the emotional bullet, but are a lot of bullets that come towards us during our age of 18 to

26 which we feel is unfair to us. But as I said in the earlier chapter, "life is just meant to be." So even maybe these bullets are meant to be and as I said let's not run from them.

In this world, we, a lot of times we will go to the city of doubts, yes here a lot of bullets will be shoots towards us and we will sometime feel helpless as some of them come from our family, or relatives, or people those a significant for us. And the more you try to dodge or run away from these bullets the more they keep coming. Because let's face it, my friend, it's family and friends. How can we run from them? And even if we do, is it the right thing to do? Is it the solution? So here we have to keep in mind not to take these bullets to heart but in fact, just start thinking and tackling it logically. There will be a lot of times when someone will doubt us or say that you cannot do it, or you will fail-this is not your cup of tea, it is during these days you have to keep moving forward even if you feel you lost a few battles.

Lose some battles

In fact, my friend I suggest losing some battles, and you will eventually - and this is the time when you will realize the difference between good and true. Yes, I have had a few people in my life who I always used to find good. Good friends, good colleagues, well-wishers, few so-called mentors. And at one place I am not the one who expects much from others when it comes to contribution to my life, but I did have some I think childish expectations from there that during the time of war they will stand for me. And no surprises here but a lot didn't. When I got into trouble I realized and they said, "They were busy," they won't be able to join. They are stuck, they have other plans and more than 158 things, in what I don't know but they were busy. And I don't have any complaint or bitterness toward such people, in fact, as I said it helped me to know the difference between good and the true ones. Losing some battles will also give us an extra minute to introspect where we exactly stand. In our own eyes, in our family's -friends- and the people whom with we spend our better times. Now here again a small catch I feel is there that "don't be bitter to these people" in the end they do have their lives and you are not on their priority list. And that is ok, my friend. You just need to be on your priority list -and that too at the top. So when you lose some battles but decide not to give up the war, you automatically become "DIY" and here is a very good chance of growth. I remember one day my mentor told me that no one is going to waste their time on you. You have got to do that yourself, if you make it worth it's not a waste of time-it is IN-VEST of time. And you have to do it yourself.

Let's TIY (Think it yourself)

When was the last time you got out of a big trouble totally by yourself?

And how does that makes you feel ?

These bullets of disappointment will also keep you humble and focused. These bullets do hurt us but they save our souls. They make us lose the battle so that we can prepare for the war. I was 19 when I started my own firm. A coaching class, and I was totally and genuinely happy with the way I was working. I was making a good impact and also making some good money. When at 23 I decided to leave, a strong bullet of emotions hit me and it was very tough for me to survive if I would have taken that bullet to my heart. So I faced and solved it logically. I know I lost a battle there, all that 4 years of hard work, the connections, and the memories went down the drain. But again it was just a battle I lost. It prepared me for the big thing. Now connecting the dots I realise that now I am making a bigger impact – a bigger contribution and in fact, once people start using this book as their tool for helping themselves, the impact and contribution will rise 100X. So I am thankful here that losing that battle didn't encourage me to quit. Yes, it hit me where it pains a lot, but it did make me the person I am today.

So again here it proves that losing a battle doesn't mean you should quit. But here you have to take care of a few things in case of preparing yourself for the war. Because some just keep throwing themselves pity parties and waste their time in greaving about what happened. And I am saying this with vast experience in doing this mistake. But my friend I never repeated it. In fact, I made sure that I keep doing things that get me ready for growth and kept myself away from the drama.

STAY AWAY FROM THE DRAMA

When we don't have good fruits or plants in our garden, people notice the grass. When we grow good plants in the garden, people enjoy the grass. So, it goes without saying, whenever you find someone who is way too much into dramatic life, who is a trouble maker in your and their own life, who loves to have drama around them- don't even wait for the red light to turn on. This is some waste and unwanted grass that will kill your energy in the long term.

I used to have a friend who was a hell of a drama person she will always be the "poor person" in the group. People used to sympathize with her. And she gets to win their attention. But was it a win for her? Was it getting her ready for the war? Was she growing? And keeping these people's company will also make you either a drama person or it will drain your energy. And then one day you - with folded hands will say I can't do this anymore. Do remember these things, my friend, "empathy over sympathy."

Leaving the dream of my life when I was 23, I realized I was broke and in trouble. I was worried and terrified with the thought of losing it out, but one good thing I did for myself was "I never seek sympathy." In fact, I hated it when someone used to show it. Because as I said I knew I have lost the battle, maybe put some people down, but I was not ready to leave, I was not ready to give up the freaking war.

Some bullets were cruel, few were unfair, and few were frustrating. But they may be a part of my life which was necessary for me to realize that losing is part of winning. Yes, read it again - connect it with your life and you will realize that it is the loss that helped you to move towards the win. Every breakup, every loss, and every bad feeling helped you to move towards better. And when you make peace with it, you make peace with your own self who is blaming yourself for things that were not in your control.

The bullet that can change you

Just think about it once, what is the most painful memory or the moment you have or are stuck in your life. Just start noticing it a bit closer, in fact, a bit deeper. The more you go deep into this memory you will realize this event or person changed you. The more emotionally connected you were – the more you changed. And again there is nothing wrong with it, but some changes will block your journey in the long run. For example, if you don't do well in a subject you started avoiding and cursing that subject more than you actually spent studying it. If you had a break-up scene you are somewhat now started keeping distance which at a point gets lonely for you. One fails business and people tend to settle for less. So this change becomes the roadblock and slows down or stops your progress. So the solution here is very simple.

The solution is very much hidden in a pizza, if by mistake, drop one piece out of 4 – you have not wasted the whole pizza, you start eating and enjoying the rest of it. So exactly like that if one area of life is not the way you wish it to be, do good and excel in the others.

Of course, I had some horrible breakups, some broke me inside out. Some business deals haunted me at night. But I knew this all is just a part of my life that will eventually leave with time, also the pain. And if I can work passionately, if I can love passionately then for sure I can live passionately. So at points, it is even ok if you have no passion for your work- or your relationships (nowadays a lot of don't) but make sure you have the passion to live and you are passionate for LIFE.

So here, the bullet of doubt just hits us so that we can start loving ourselves more than we love someone else. We enjoy our time the way we do with others.

In simple words, be your first and the most important priority.

Losing some battles also made me realize the real meaning of winning. And how important for us to keep going when the odds are totally against us.

During the graduation, I met a lot of people who turned out to be friends and then today again strangers. But I don't remember having a fight or any hard feelings towards these people. Then why they are no more a part of my life and why I am not bothered about theirs. The answer here is very simple my friend "some people are just temporary in our life, and even for us we are there to play a temporary role." So make sure you play your role best for them. These people, some of them will play a very important role during a few of your battles but won't be there during the big war. Some will decide to leave, some will stay till the end. In every way, you should not stop. You should keep going.

During the workshops, I have met a lot of people and some are still in touch with me. Some share festival messages, and birthday wishes, and some do call and ask about health and life. But at the same time, some moved in their life, and I never got to see how are they doing. But again, we have to keep going right.

So, my dear friend, one of the important keys during these years of war in our life is to be your own partner first and consciously decide to keep moving. Remember at points friends will maybe leave – don't be bitter with them, after all, they have their own battles. Maybe the family will somewhere stop their support - again they have their own life to live. So don't complain if you find yourself alone during some battles, and don't worry if you lose some. Because in the end, my friend, I know I have lost some battles – but I am blessed that I lived the war. And this MANTRA, after hearing it from"Sudha Murti Ji"became my go-to place during these hard times when we are living the WAR.

Here I am sharing some of my learnings during the WAR and when I am stuck in it alone, but did manage to survive and kept going.

1. Your dreams and goals are totally your responsibility and if you are waiting for somebody to give you permission, or to discover you, or to pick you up, I've got news for you my friend: NO ONE'S COMING.

2. You need to kick your own ass and stop waiting for the perfect time, the perfect plan, and the perfect moment. What you need is to kick your own ass because the universe rewards people who take risks, not those who only play it safe. So if you, my friend, want to change your life, you need to be the hero of your story.

3. You don't need permission – you need to take action because here's the truth my friend: the people in life who get what they want are the ones that aren't waiting for an external force to validate their

dreams, inspire them, or give them permission. In fact, it's the people that realize that success, happiness, and control come from an internal force, and that is "YOU. "

4. Even if you don't feel ready, do it anyway because you are never going to feel ready. You're never going to find the perfect time. You'll always feel nervous right before you start. You won't have all the answers. And yes, you are going to screw up a few times. But my friend, DO IT ANYWAY.

5. Remember my friend big changes happen with small daily actions so do one thing that moves you in the direction of your GOALS.

6. If you're outside your comfort zone, you're doing it right and as you start really working toward the things that you really want to do, you're not going to feel ready. You're going to feel outside of your comfort zone. And it will drive you crazy at some point. A lot of times you will feel useless and worthless. And my friend THAT'S NORMAL. When you start to feel like you're stretching yourself, and you're sticking your neck out there, and you're taking some risks, that's amazing because my friend you're GROWING.

7. Repeat, yes repeat. Remember you have to do it. No one is coming to discover you, find you, date you, or rescue you. It's your life and your responsibility. It's your goals and they are your responsibility. And here the only person whose permission you need is your OWN.

    This is what I have learned from the time I was wandering during these days of the war. The war sometimes breaks us throughout and sometimes makes us the HULK. So don't be afraid of losing some battles, yeah I was in fear, confusion, and self-doubt, but now when look back I just look up and repeat "I know I have lost some battles- but I live the war."

Notes:

Someday It Will All Be Worth It

Someday it will all be worth it. The hard work, the rejections, the breakups, the sleepless nights, and the urge to give but the will go keep going, some day it will all be worth it.

Every person of whatsoever age just wakeup and even go to bed with this exact same thought. That someday all this will be worth it and life will be finally, you know LIFE. Not a bad thing to start your day and I believe the best one to end the day with. But again life is not just what you think during the first 10 minutes or what you repeat before you sleep. Life is what you do between these both, of course, morning manifestation is good -I suggest it to almost every participant of mine. But the life we want and the life we have makes a difference in what we do between this. Every entrepreneur I read or watched about have just one thing in common – they dreamt about it when they sleep, they repeated it once they woke up, but they kept hustling on every other opportunity they got. And my friend just as morning and night – we get opportunities daily. So what you do during this is what will make it happen. In some previous chapters, we have learned about or at least read about the mindset, the sense of achievement and appreciation, the relationship glass, and how the key works for our success. Here in this chapter, we are going to talk about the hustle and the never ending things it takes for maybe someday to be worth it. I have had a lot of sleepless nights when I was even trying to work, and when I started the actual work I realized it takes a lot of things to make it happen. But before I share this chapter with you –let's take a ride to the city of change – let's go where it all started – let's go down the memory lane, but remember, my friend, "past is a very nice place to visit off but a very wrong one to stay for long."

So I was 17, happy go lucky, carefree, and a lot of time careless. But ultimately happy. I had no passion for money or any lavish lifestyle. I didn't even know what it takes to make money. I just thought that one day when the college and educational years will be done, a job- a good pay job will pop out for me. I used to think I will get a very well-paid job with a good designation, I will marry the girl I love, my family will be proud and happy with me, and I will be the centre of the universe- at least my universe. And day by day my careless attitude started building up. But I still remember the day when I was having a word with my father and he told me his earnings. As I said I was 17, before that day I never knew how much my dad used to earn, how he managed to get 2 stubborn kids well educated and how was he paying all the bills, how he managed to get us those things during festivals, and lastly, I didn't know that during all these years of his life, he is been working just so that we can lead a good life in our future.

Now today, I am a double graduate and may have more than 10 certificates in what I do, but still, I consider myself less educated as a person than he is. Because of that day the 17 years young I realized,

"We were not rich" and he is trying his every way to make it happen. So, my friend, when our parents work their entire life off just so that we can lead a wonderful life- we are supposed to make it happen RIGHT? Or else what will it be worth it for them? What did they work so hard for? Why should even they compromise for something they worked for so hard and we are just lucky to get in, even if not on a silver platter, I will say I am lucky to get it. Yes, my parents have worked hard so that I can have a life I will be proud of and they will be too. So that day, as a 17-year-old, gave a hit my mind that I will make it happen. I will make all their sleepless nights, the situations where they must have decided to quit but because or for me they didn't, I will make all those things that they sacrificed just for me – I WILL MAKE ALL OF IT worth it. And that will be my biggest gift to them, the biggest gift as a child. But more importantly, that will be the right and deserving tribute I can give to their hard work.

So, dear friend, I know I was careless – but I was never worthless, no one is. So I decided to change what I don't like. When we don't like the shirt we are wearing we change it, when we don't like our shoes or watch or hairstyle – we change it. So then if we don't like the life we are living we have all the right to CHANGE IT. And changes not only happen during the night or with the morning manifestation. But changes also take place when we decide to make opportunities count. See I don't know about KARMA, I don't know if God has ever listened to my prayers or my early morning affirmations. But I know he is watching me working. He is watching me working with people who I know are helping me to grow, he is watching me when I am down in life. And he watched me during these years when I have left my comfort zone to my people comfortable.

So yes, just like others, I have been working hard, I have made some sacrifices, I won some battles -I lost some. I got my heart broken by someone I loved. I left a few places I used to be in love with. I left the old me so that I can welcome the new ME. And I am not ashamed of the battles I lost, or the people who have rejected me, even people who have surpassed me and got what I wanted. Because my friend I believe some day – IT ALL WILL BE WORTH IT, even if not for me – but for the hard work my family did for me.

So as I said, "PAST IS A VERY NICE PLACE TO VISIT, AND A VERY WRONG ONE TO STAY FOR LONG." Let's come back to the chapter and the activities that will help us make all of it WORTH IT.

Remember, we are doing what we are doing to make it happen. But do we know what we want to happen? And who will help us to get there? And who will stand with us if we fail? And who will drag us down? And and and and? And there are a lot of questions that we sometimes don't know the answers to. But again, we can give it a shot. There is no harm in giving it a shot for sure. So, my friend, here I am sharing an activity for you that may help you to know and move towards what you really want.

Do this and then go and work for it. Because life is as we have seen in the earlier chapters "DO IT YOURSELF."

And in this journey where we all are waiting for the day where all this seems worth it, FAITH plays a very important role. Yes, it does, but there are a few more learning or realizations we all need to get through the tough times and make it happen. I learned this may be a hard way, but this book and especially this chapter will be there to help you, my friend. So make sure you read it quietly, understand it deeply and then make it worth the hard work and sacrifice for it.

1. **No one has it all figured out,** and everybody is wandering in their own way.
2. **To love is to be vulnerable, so let your guard down.** We all know that a ship is safe at the shore than in the ocean, but it is not made to stay at the shore. Is it? So let your guard down when you love someone – yes you run the chances of getting hurt but you will never be able to love purely with all your guards holding you.
3. **Good or bad, you can learn from everyone.** We, my friend, are a magnet we are going to attract both good and bad. It's our decision-making and awareness that will help us to keep the GOOD and let go of what's bad for us.
4. **Embrace your emotions, all of them, don't ignore them, don't mask them up, and just embrace them.** I learned this a very hard way that the more you try to stop your emotions, the more you get terrified of them. You tend to lose your capability of feeling in the moment. And at

some point, you lose to feel what's going on inside you. And that is not a very good thing to do. Emotions are natural. They deserve to be embraced and our attention even if some of them hurt us for a while.

5. **Maturity is accepting you won't get answers to the things that hurt you the most-** you should heal anyway. As a teenager, I never got answers to my some relationships ended the way they took off. I didn't get the answers to why at points I used to feel that my castle of life is been built of pillars of soil or sand. Why one minute I was winning and the other I struggled to make things happen. But I actually started healing when I decided not to find answers for all the things that happened to or with me.

6. **One day my friend you will need to be forgiven –** so learn to forgive first. Be so big to learn to forgive the people who may be at some time have hurt you. Forgiving someone doesn't mean being in touch or trusting blindly. Some forgiveness is just for making peace with that part of life. So learn to forgive and move forward, don't cling to what and how and why it happened.

7. **Listen to understand, not just to respond-** at a point in my life I did felt I have been misunderstood or being targeted. But the day I started to listen to people just to understand and not to respond, I got to know the real ones. Also, listen to understand because nowadays a lot of

people you meet are said to be on their own. So helping them heal will also help you to heal yourself at any given time.

8. **Remember that 80% of the success in any job is based on your ability to deal with people.** We as humans are social animals and we all want to enjoy good friendships, good relationships, and good people around us. But nowadays the biggest challenge people face is that they are suffering to make their relationships work. They at some point fail to deal with people because of the fear of getting judged by them and a lot of time because of rejection.

9. **You can't pour from an empty cup.** Take care of yourself first- a lot of times we do the mistake of not keeping ourselves at prior. The challenge here is what we discussed in the chapter of GLASS HALF FULL, and once we get drained off we start feeling worthless and lonely. So the suggestion here is that the next time you start feeling worthless, fill your half with good and important things in your life.

So my friend these are the 9 learnings I have had from those days when I am trying to make it all worthwhile and I believe they will help you.

The question here while we are doing this is to whom we are trying to show or prove that all this will make sense and be worth it someday? Because the people who really care about your happiness and growth will care for it and stand by you, others –won't. I have been told a lot of times that when it will all work out – we will be there to celebrate. But then what if it doesn't? What if I fail? Or do I fail miserably? What about days when I am down? So, my friend, a lot of time you will have people to celebrate and not support. A lot of time you will hear the sound of "CHEERS for you "but not "DON'T WORRY – I AM THERE – AND WE WILL FIGURE THIS OUT." What about those days my friend?

You will feel depressed, sometimes you will feel the walls closing on you, and sometimes you will feel like falling down a mountain of expectations. What about those days?

So here I am sharing with you how I bounced back from depression by overcoming my habit of procrastination and prioritization. Yes, it has helped me during those days of the war I had to fight on my own.

"You see, procrastination isn't just something we're doing because we're "bored". Once you learn the simple truth of where it comes from and why you do it, it dissolves almost instantly and you almost forget how to waste time ever again. It works by first discovering your "procrastination type" and then letting the changes unfold naturally.

Here I am sharing an ANTI PROCRASTINATION DAILY ROUTINE with you which you can use to solve this issue.

The Planner – Now here first plan your day hour by hour. Do deep work for 2 hours with zero distractions. Take a stretching break every now and then or once you complete a particular task. When feeling overwhelmed work on the lighter tasks. Plan how you will celebrate once you complete a particular task or goal. Then make sure you repeat this cycle at least 2 times a day.

The Prioritizer- Write a to-do list for yourself. Start by organizing your calendar. Do the hardest task first so that you can have a sense of achievement when you do the other. Also, prioritize your health first and things that for real help you grow. When feeling overwhelmed do the favorite thing or talk to a favorite person at that moment.

The Arranger- Arrange yourself, your home, your table, your closet, and the things you use the most. Start writing a journal or note of the day-just brain dump your thoughts on a paper, if they are useful keep them, if not we all have a dustbin at our place for a reason. Work on more challenging tasks and when feeling overwhelmed try clearing your mobile gallery. You will enjoy it.

The Visualizer- As it is said, if you can visualize it- you can do it & and if you can do it once you can achieve it. So, decide on a priority for the day. Write about the goals and tasks. Sometimes even the outcome you want. End the day with light tasks and if you ever hit the bottom- VISUALIZE your favorite person or event.

Day by day while doing this I realized that depression can be cured even by anti-procrastination. Because once you get things going their natural way with your conscious effort – it all feels to be worth it.

In the journey of making it happen, you will hit some roadblocks. Some will be easy to cross – some will be a pain for you. Some will even scream in years "GIVE UP" and you will feel that it's time. It's time you should even stop trying. So yeah, even I say GIVE UP, but with a little change. If you are on a verge of giving up just for once try this and see how your life gets back on track.

1. Give up sticking to the person you used to be – step outside of the person you have been for a while. Remember who you want to be and what you are capable of. Stop demoting yourself and grow and improve if you have to come out of your comfort zone, do it happily for the person you want to.

2. Stop and give up criticising yourself for everything you aren't – you are your first love, love yourself in thoughts, words, and actions. Be kind to yourself my friend. Believe me, it is more important than being kind to others. While learning how to do new things in life, learn to work through your fears, insecurities, and anger. While doing things for others make

sure you help yourself to grow beyond pity things. Grow because you deserve it.

3. Give up regretting and holding on to your past – because when you hold to your past, you miss the beauty of the present. And there is just one time you are growing and that is the present. So enjoy what you have today while working on what you want to achieve for tomorrow. Some things didn't work out in the past so that you will have room for some in the present.

4. Give up getting caught up in the negativity surrounding you because it is essential to keep your state positive even in some negative situations. If you keep looking for the worst in things and people, it destroys your capacity to do your best. So ACT positively, even in some small way, and don't sit and wait for a perfect future.

5. Give up thinking that others' life is much easier because nothing worthwhile is ever easy and everyone around you faces their struggles, and it is hard as it is for you. So don't think that the grass is greener on the other side.

6. Give up wanting to be where others' are in life and stop comparing where you are at with where everybody else is. It doesn't take you forward. It pulls you down. Remember, my friend, you are different than others, and so are your goals, dreams, and journey. But you have to trust that you are in the right place at the given time. This is your best version for the

given time, yeah there is always room for improvement.

7. Give up letting the judgement of others control you because others don't know your story and what you have been through. So what you think about yourself is what matters the most. So think about yourself and do what is right for you and not what others think you should be doing.

8. Give up believing you aren't strong enough to move forward – it's always possible to go on, no matter how impossible it might seem. My friend, just remember and believe someday it will all be worth it so dare to take one more step. Be your biggest investment and one day you be glad that you did it.

9. Give up overthinking and worrying as it only creates problems that are not present in the first place. Worrying takes away today's peace and potential-but, not tomorrows' troubles.

In our life, a lot of times we feel that giving up is way much easier than keeping going, and this is the point we should think about what we can give up to save our goal, energy, and soul.

Write down 5 habits that you will give up from today for the next 21 days to help you to make it all worth it.

1. ________________________________

2. _______________________________
3. _______________________________
4. _______________________________
5. _______________________________

Before we end this chapter, my friend, I will like to share a simple message with you that I learned from my mentor. "Struggle is personal, it doesn't have to make sense to others." You go through a lot of things, make a lot of sacrifices, and go through a lot of heartbreaks to make it worth it. Just make sure you -yourself never GIVE UP. Because remember, my friend, no matter how hard it has been and how hard it is being right now- ONE DAY IT WILL ALL BE WORTH IT.

Notes:

You Are a Package

My friend, you have done it. You have come this far and this shows that you belong to that 1% of the people who believe in taking action to achieve what you desire. Now we are all set to end this journey you have started on a very light but very important note.

You are a package, a combo one, a sizzler, or like a jumbo meal that comes with fires and some good shake to drink. Just like it, you also are a package, you also come up with a lot of things, qualities, habits, values, thoughts, and plans. But a lot of people just wander by themselves and be totally unaware of what kind of package they are. So here in this last and short chapter let us see what kind of package you are. Because once you yourself know what kind of package you are and what you bring to the table no one can demotivate you and no one can put things in your mind. Here you become self-dependable and not on others.

So here are some questions I asked a few of my participants and these questions will help you to get a very good visual realization of yourself. A lot of people never think about themselves this way and therefore are unaware of their SUPERPOWERS and NOT so SUPERPOWERS so they keep wasting their time and energy. Let's start with the questions

1.   If you are a package which one do you think you are? Also, write why?
        i) Diamond
        ii) Gold
        iii) Silver
        iv) Bronze

2.   If you are a package, how many stars you will give to yourself? Also, write why?
        i) 5 stars
        ii) 4 stars
        iii) 3stars
        iv) 2 stars
        v) 1 star

3.   If you are a package with what terms and conditions you may come?

____

____

____

____

____

____

____

____

____

____

4.   If you are a package, is there any special condition you will come with?

____

____

____

____

____

____

5.   If you are a package what kind of people will be comfortable with you?

____

____

____

____

____

____

6.   What are the top 5 Values you as a package has?

     1. _______________________

     2. _______________________

     3. _______________________

     4. _______________________

     5. _______________________

7.   What are the top 5 complaints people may have from you as a package?

     1. _______________________

     2. _______________________

     3. _______________________

     4. _______________________

     5. _______________________

8.   What are the top 5 reasons people should trust you as a package?

     1. _______________________

     2. _______________________

     3. _______________________

     4. _______________________

     5. _______________________

9.   What are the top 5 Improvements you need as a package?

     1. _______________________

     2. _______________________

     3. _______________________

     4. _______________________

5. _______________________________

10.   How you as a package can bring the special change out in the universe?
1. _______________________________
2. _______________________________
3. _______________________________
4. _______________________________
5. _______________________________

Now here, be honest with yourself and your qualities. Do your best on working on the mission "GROWTH" and start working on project "YOURSELF."

During my teenage, one very important thing I have realized is, "when we start working on ourselves – everyone starts working on us." The moment we avoid ourselves, so do the people." So during my 21st age, I made my life DIY and stopped being dependent on others for the majority of my work.

I started working on project ME and stopped a lot of unnecessary things and topic which no longer serves towards my growth. Of course, political comments or traffic issues stopped bothering me and my health, income, education, relations, and how much knowledge I have on my NICHE are what mattered.

So my friend, AGE 21 or AGE 91 – all this is just what we make out of it, our values, habits, goals, people we keep as a company, movies we watch the books we read are majorly responsible for it. I hope the activities in the book and the questions will help you to connect with yourself and help to become the version of yourself you should be and for what you came into the world because, my friend, as I started the book with the reason of

Each person comes into this world with a specific destiny – he has something to fulfill, some message to be delivered, and some work has to be completed. You are not here accidentally – you are here meaningfully. There is a purpose behind you. The whole intends to do something through you.

- Osho (1931-1990) Indian mystic

I believe each of us have the capacity to make the magic happen and grow without limit.

Because in life - our life, sometimes we look for something and find something else. But the universe makes sure that we find the right thing. So trust yourself and keep moving forward.

Notes: